LIVING TRUST & ESTATE PLANNING

THE ALL-IN-ONE SOLUTION TO BUILD A LIVING TRUST, ORGANIZE YOUR ESTATE, CUT COSTS, SAVE ON TAXES, AND LEAVE A SMOOTH, SECURE FINANCIAL FUTURE FOR YOUR LOVED ONES

LUCAS STERLING

TOP TIER PRESS

Published under the author brand **Lucas Sterling**

This edition contains material originally published separately as:

Book One: *Estate Planning* © 2025 Top Tier Press

Book Two: *Living Trusts* © 2025 Top Tier Press

CONTENTS

PART ONE
ESTATE PLANNING

PART TWO
LIVING TRUSTS

PART ONE
ESTATE PLANNING

HOW TO ORGANIZE YOUR ASSETS, SAVE THOUSANDS IN LEGAL COSTS, CREATE A LIVING TRUST, AND PASS ON YOUR LEGACY WITHOUT LEGAL HEADACHES WITH THIS STEP-BY-STEP PLAN

INTRODUCTION

Few topics generate more discomfort—and more confusion—than estate planning. For many adults, it conjures images of mahogany offices, stacks of legal documents, and the wealthy brooding over family fortunes. Too often, the question of a will, trust, or power of attorney is quietly pushed aside, dismissed as something to tackle "someday," or assumed unnecessary unless you have vast assets or are approaching retirement. But here's the truth: estate planning isn't just for the rich, the elderly, or those with complicated financial portfolios. It's for everyone who cares about protecting what matters most—your loved ones, your home, your hard-earned savings, and your peace of mind.

If you're reading this, chances are you're not alone in feeling uncertain about where to begin. Maybe you're a parent wanting to ensure your children are cared for if the unthinkable happens. Perhaps you own a home or have started building savings and want to know how to prevent legal headaches for your family down the line. You might be caring for aging parents and are becoming all too aware of the challenges that come when someone passes without a plan. Or perhaps you've witnessed the emotional and financial turmoil left in the wake of a loved one's passing, wishing there had been better preparation. No matter what stage of life you're at, estate planning can help you take control, reduce stress, and leave a positive legacy.

Let's start by busting a persistent myth: estate planning is not reserved for millionaires, retirees, or people with sprawling investment accounts. In reality, most families—middle-income earners, first-time homeowners, single parents, blended families, and even young professionals just starting to build wealth—stand to benefit the most from having a clear plan in place. In fact, the absence of planning can have the greatest impact on people who can least afford unexpected legal costs or prolonged uncertainty.

Consider this: What would happen if something occurred to you tomorrow? Who would make decisions about your health care or finances if you couldn't speak for yourself? How quickly could your loved ones access your accounts or manage your property? Without a legally valid estate plan, the answers to these questions shift away from your family's wishes and into the hands of state laws and courts. The process is called probate—a lengthy and often expensive legal ordeal that can freeze assets, create delays, and impose significant court fees. Even simple cases can stretch on for months, requiring family members to navigate paperwork, hearings, and government bureaucracy at a time when they may already be overwhelmed by grief.

The lack of an estate plan doesn't just create legal obstacles; it can also lead to painful family disputes, lost savings, and irreparable relationships. Imagine siblings arguing over parental possessions, spouses unable to access bank accounts, or caregivers struggling to pay bills or make urgent medical decisions because proper documents weren't in place. These situations aren't rare—they play out in families every single day, regardless of income level or background. Many people don't realize that their "modest" estate, which includes a house, some savings, retirement accounts, and sentimental belongings, still requires careful planning to ensure it reaches the appropriate beneficiaries efficiently and safely.

But this book isn't written to scare you—it's written to empower you. Taking control of your estate plan now is one of the greatest gifts you can give yourself and those you love. Planning ahead provides clarity, saves time and money, and ensures your choices—not a judge's or state government's—determine what happens if life takes an unexpected turn. Having a well-thought-out estate plan provides you with the assurance that your family won't struggle to find solutions in times of need. It allows you to specify guardians for your children, select trusted individuals to handle your affairs, protect vulnerable family members, and pass on your values along with your assets. Even better, getting started is far less daunting than you might think. With the right guidance, clear steps, and modern tools, creating or updating an estate plan can be straightforward and affordable—even if you don't hire an expensive attorney.

This book is your roadmap through the estate planning process, designed specifically for everyday people—not just lawyers or the ultra-wealthy. Whether you're a parent, homeowner, caregiver, retiree, or simply someone who values a secure future, you'll find practical advice tailored to your circumstances. We'll break down complex concepts using plain language and real-world examples, helping you cut through legal jargon and zero in on what actually matters. You'll learn:

- Why every adult should have key documents in place—regardless of age, marital status, or net worth.
- How to set up a simple, cost-effective estate plan that meets your needs and fits your budget.
- Steps for choosing guardians, executors, and decision-makers you trust.
- Strategies to avoid common pitfalls like probate delays, court battles, and unnecessary legal bills.
- Tips on updating your plan as your life evolves, from marriage and parenthood to divorce, second marriages, or changing assets.

- Special considerations for blended families, business owners, and caregivers managing aging parents' estates.
- Ways to communicate your wishes and foster family harmony before and after you're gone.

You may feel overwhelmed or uncertain about where to begin, and that's completely normal. Estate planning often feels unfamiliar, technical, and emotionally charged. The good news? Once you understand the essentials, each step becomes manageable—and the sense of relief you'll feel is well worth the effort. This book will walk you through the process one chapter at a time, offering checklists, explanations, and sample scenarios to guide your decisions.

Remember, estate planning isn't about focusing on worst-case scenarios. It's about proactively shaping the future for yourself and those you care about, ensuring your hard work and values live on. It's about sparing your family needless frustration, saving money that would otherwise go to legal fees, and making sure the things you cherish end up in the right hands. It's about making your voice heard, no matter what tomorrow brings.

No matter your age, relationship status, or financial situation, taking charge of your estate plan is an act of responsibility—and of love. You don't need to be wealthy or ready to retire. You simply need the desire to safeguard your future and look out for the people closest to you. Let's erase the barriers, replace confusion with clarity, and get you on track to building a plan that truly reflects your wishes. The journey starts now.

UNLOCK YOUR ESTATE PLANNING & LIVING TRUST COMPANION WORKBOOK

Ready to turn your estate planning goals into clarity, confidence, and lasting peace of mind?

As a thank-you for reading this book, I've created a helpful companion resource: **The Estate Planning & Living Trust Companion Workbook.** This practical guide helps you organize documents, define your legacy, and create a trust that reflects your values. It's designed to take you from uncertainty to assurance in just a few thoughtful steps.

What's included in this resource:

- Clarify your estate planning goals
- Organize and record key information and assets
- Simplify trust creation and beneficiary planning
- Protect your loved ones and ensure your wishes are honored

👉 **Access Your Companion Workbook**
Visit: **https://content.toptierpress.com/simplify-planning-journey**

Or scan the QR code below to get instant access!

CHAPTER 1

ESTATE PLANNING BASICS – WHAT, WHY, AND WHEN

Estate planning is often misunderstood as something only necessary for the wealthy or elderly, but this belief overlooks its true purpose and broad relevance. Regardless of your age or income, having a clear plan in place ensures that your wishes are respected, your loved ones are cared for, and potential legal complications are minimized. Many people delay these important decisions because the topic feels complicated or intimidating, yet putting off estate planning can lead to confusion and conflict when unexpected events occur.

This chapter breaks down estate planning into simple, understandable terms and explains why it matters to anyone with assets or dependents. It guides you through the key concepts and shows how making thoughtful choices now can save your family time, money, and stress later. By understanding the essentials, you'll gain confidence to take control of your future and the security to protect what matters most.

Understanding Estate Planning & Key Terms

Planning what happens to your property, money, and responsibilities isn't just for the wealthy or the elderly. Estate planning helps you make decisions about how your belongings and care will be managed both during your life and after you pass away. It allows you to protect what matters most, reduce confusion, spare loved ones from difficult choices, and ensure your wishes are clear in advance. For a young parent, this might mean choosing a trusted guardian for their children. For a homeowner, it could involve deciding who will inherit the family house or how any debts will be handled. Even for someone with modest possessions, estate planning lightens the burden on friends and family by giving them clear guidance during a difficult time.

Estate planning includes more than a single document or decision. It brings together several elements that work as one. A central piece is the will. Think of a will as a written set of instructions explaining where your belongings should go, who will care for your children, and who will oversee your plans. For example, if you collect coins and want your nephew to have them, your will ensures that wish is honored. If you have children under eighteen, naming a guardian can prevent family disputes or court involvement later.

Next, there's the trust. Imagine a trust as a locked box holding money or property. You set the rules by deciding who gets the key, who benefits, and when things are given out. With a trust, a parent can make sure a child inherits money only once they reach a certain age, or they can help a family member with disabilities receive support long-term. A trust can also limit taxes and avoid long legal steps for your loved ones.

Estate does not mean a grand mansion. Your estate includes everything you own—your home, car, jewelry, bank accounts, and even pets. If you have a plant collection or a beloved cat, these are part of your estate. Estate planning makes sure each piece ends up where you want.

Probate is the legal process that happens after you die, when your estate is sorted, debts are paid, and what's left goes to the people you selected. This process can take a long time and sometimes costs money. For instance, if you leave a will naming your sister to receive your record collection, probate makes that official. Having a will or trust can shorten or even skip the probate process.

Every plan needs someone to see it through. That's the executor. An executor is like the team captain of your estate, making sure your instructions are followed. If you choose your best friend to be executor, he or she will collect belongings, pay off your bills from your bank account, and hand out your possessions as directed in your will.

A beneficiary is anyone you choose to receive something from your estate. These might be family, friends, charities, or anyone important to you. For example, Anna leaves her childhood books to her niece and a donation to her favorite animal shelter—the niece and the shelter are beneficiaries.

Here's how all these pieces connect. The estate is what you own. The will lists your wishes and names an executor, who's in charge. The executor collects what's in your estate, pays any debts, and gives your belongings to the beneficiaries named in your will. If you have a trust, the person managing it (the trustee) follows your instructions by handing out assets in the time and way that you set. Probate is the system that checks everything that happens legally. Each step helps your loved ones manage the business of loss with fewer complications and less stress.

Being prepared with an estate plan is not about how much money you have or how old you are. It is about helping those you care for when you cannot be there yourself. Creating a plan gives you greater control, saves your family extra trouble, and makes tough times easier to handle. The next step grows from this sense of protection and clarity—knowing when to act and what tools fit your needs the best. This awareness shows why starting sooner can make a difference no matter your age or financial situation, setting the stage for the choices ahead.

Why Estate Planning Matters and When to Start

Clarity about what a will does, or what an executor manages, takes estate planning out of the realm of abstract paperwork and makes its uses feel real. Understanding that a will allows you to designate who inherits the house, and that a power of attorney ensures bills are paid while you're in the hospital, is important for real families. Estate planning is not a task saved for wealthy or older people; it's for anyone with something or someone to protect. Every parent who sets up a guardian for their child, or every homeowner who wants to prevent heirs from fighting over who gets what, uses estate planning tools rooted in those basic terms. A will is just the start of deciding who takes care of your family and what becomes of your home. For those caring for aging parents, documents like powers of attorney help families carry out a loved one's wishes smoothly, sidestepping frustration and confusion.

Some myths stand in the way of prompt and useful estate planning. Many people believe estate planning only applies to those with large bank accounts, vacation homes, or valuable stocks. In fact, if you have a bank account at all, a car, treasured personal possessions, or a story about how a family memento almost got lost after a funeral, estate planning concerns you. Some hold off, reasoning, "I'm too young," or "I'll get to it when I've built up more savings." Yet, life events rarely follow a neat timeline. Illness, accidents, or sudden changes can upend plans at any stage. Imagine a young couple with a new baby—unexpected events could leave a child's care in limbo unless a will names a guardian. Homeowners who wait to spell out who inherits their property may leave families scrambling in probate court, fighting over who owns the house or how it gets divided. Even adult children managing affairs for aging parents sometimes find themselves locked out of accounts or unable to step in when there's no plan on file.

Estate planning gives families a sense of order and security. It shrinks the risk of arguments over property, keeps sensitive health decisions from falling to strangers or the courts, and can keep costs low by helping people avoid long, expensive legal processes. Few things cause more stress in hard times than not knowing what to do or who gets to decide for someone who can no longer speak for themselves. Taking time to make basic choices now gives everyone a firmer footing when unexpected events arrive.

Major life events are the best moments to create or update an estate plan. These include:

- Getting married or entering a partnership
- Getting divorced or separated
- Having a child or adopting
- Buying or selling property, such as a house or land
- Facing a health diagnosis, injury, or major surgery
- Starting or closing a business
- Inheriting money or property from someone else

Your plan should be reviewed, as these changes can alter your possessions or who you protect. A sensible rule is to check your estate plan every few years or when something important shifts in your life. Outdated documents may name incorrect people, leave out new children or grandchildren, or refer to property you no longer own. Keeping your plan up to date helps avoid confusion and gives your family what they need.

Getting started is not as hard as it seems. Begin with a list of everything you own and who you'd want to receive it. Write down things like bank and retirement accounts, your house, a car, jewelry, or personal keepsakes. Make another list of people you trust to handle your affairs if something happens: potential guardians for children, backup decision-makers, or friends who know you well. Gather critical paperwork—property deeds, account statements, insurance policies, titles, and any prior wills or legal agreements. Use a checklist or worksheet to keep things organized and avoid missing important steps.

No one's plan will be perfect on the first try. The best action is to make a start now, putting basic choices on paper and updating them as life goes on. Changes can always be made later as your situation and wishes evolve. This simple, direct approach moves estate planning from something overwhelming to something manageable. By starting early, you give your family clarity, confidence, and protection from avoidable trouble. These first steps help you learn how to manage your estate.

Building Your Foundation: A Clear Recap

A robust estate plan provides comfort to individuals seeking to safeguard their assets and provide for their loved ones. It's not just about who gets what; it's about making your wishes known, handling your assets as you want, and protecting your dependents from confusion or conflict. An estate plan puts you in the driver's seat, giving you a clear say over what happens to your property, finances, and even your personal care when you can no longer make those decisions yourself.

At the center of estate planning is the will, a legal document that lists exactly how your assets—money, property, and possessions—should be given out after you're gone. The will is also where parents can name guardians for minor children, a step that gives lasting security to families in unexpected situations. Without a will, state law decides who gets what, and relatives may face delays and disagreements.

Another central term is trust. A trust is a way to set aside assets so that a trustee, a person or institution you pick, can manage them for a beneficiary. For example, you might set up a trust so your children receive their inheritance at a certain age or for safe management of money for someone with special needs. Trusts help avoid probate, keep financial details private, and offer flexibility in how and when assets are distributed. They can be a smart choice when families want to prevent disputes by spelling out the rules beforehand.

Probate is the court process that happens when someone dies and their will needs to be carried out. Probate gathers the person's assets, pays debts and bills, and makes sure property is passed on according to their wishes as written in the will. This process can take months or even longer, and the costs can eat into the estate. A careful estate plan can help keep probate simple or, in some cases, avoid it altogether.

Every will needs an executor. This is the person who handles the details—filing the will, dealing with debts, paying taxes, and distributing property. The executor is a trusted helper who follows the instructions in your plan. Deciding who should take this role is a major part of making your estate plan work smoothly.

The people or organizations who inherit assets from a will or trust are called beneficiaries. These might be loved ones, friends, or charities. Stating clearly who the beneficiaries are makes your plan clear and avoids hurt feelings or arguments.

Estate planning offers many benefits that reach beyond just distributing money or property. It reduces the chance of family disputes, makes sure minor children and dependents are supported, and gives you the chance to set out medical or financial wishes in case you're no longer able to express them directly. For instance, naming a guardian in your will ensures that children will have a stable home, rather than leaving the decision to courts or relatives who might disagree. Putting property in a trust can give adult children access to funds at a steady pace, which helps avoid wasteful spending or fights among siblings.

The best time to create or update an estate plan isn't limited to one's later years. Any adult who owns assets—or who has children or other people relying on them—needs a plan. Big life moments give you a reason to take action or make changes. Key events that should prompt you to review your plan include:

- Marriage or divorce
- Birth or adoption of a child
- Buying or selling a major asset like a house or business
- Retirement
- Major changes in health, finances, or family relationships

A good estate plan isn't a single event, but an ongoing process that keeps pace with your life. Even if you made a plan years ago, revisiting it after any major change is wise. This way, your wishes—and the well-being of those you care about—stay protected.

Taking action begins with a few clear steps. Listing out what you own, from bank accounts to family heirlooms, gives you a full picture of your estate. Thinking through who you trust most to act as an executor or trustee ensures capable, honest management. Talking with loved ones about your goals turns your wishes into a shared understanding and can prevent confusion when the time comes.

Choosing to handle estate planning now puts you in control. With this knowledge, you can move forward with purpose, clear direction, and the confidence that your wishes—and those you love—are well cared for.

Main Points Recap

Now that you understand the key elements of estate planning and why it matters for people at every stage of life, you can take confident steps toward securing your future and protecting those you care about most. By starting early and keeping your plan current, you reduce stress, avoid unnecessary legal hurdles, and give your family clear instructions when they need them most. Whether you're safeguarding a home, naming guardians for children, or ensuring your wishes are honored, this knowledge empowers you to make thoughtful choices with clarity and control. Moving forward, use these insights as a foundation to build or update your estate plan—transforming what once seemed complex into a manageable process that offers peace of mind today and tomorrow.

CHAPTER 2

TAKING INVENTORY – WHAT YOU OWN AND WHAT YOU OWE

More than half of Americans don't have a clear list of their assets and debts when it comes time to plan their estate. This lack of organization can lead to confusion, delays, and unexpected costs for families trying to settle affairs during difficult times. Without a clear picture of what you own and what you owe, even simple tasks like paying bills or transferring property can become complicated and stressful for those left behind. By taking the initial step to inventory your financial life, you can gain control and clarity, which in turn lays the foundation for seamless planning and peace of mind. This chapter begins that essential process—helping you create a straightforward map of your financial world so you and your loved ones avoid unnecessary challenges down the road.

Cataloging Your Assets and Liabilities

Breaking your financial world into assets and liabilities gives you a clear starting point for estate planning. This approach provides real control over your affairs and ensures that nothing is overlooked. Take out a notebook and create two pages: one labeled **"What You Own"** and the other **"What You Owe."** The more accurate and organized your records are now, the fewer complications your loved ones will face later.

Begin with assets. List everything you own that has value, grouping items by category. The most straightforward assets are your bank and savings accounts. Record the name of each bank, the type of account (checking, savings, certificate of deposit), the account holder's name, and an approximate balance. If you share an account with a spouse, parent, or someone else, note whether it's **joint** or **individual.** For example: *John and Lisa – Checking account, First State Bank, Joint, $3,200.*

Next, move to retirement savings. Include IRAs, 401(k)s, company pensions, and similar plans. Note which accounts you own individually and which are shared. Record the financial institution and estimate the current value. For example: *Lisa's 401(k), Widget Corp, Individual owner, $86,000.* These accounts are often among the most valuable parts of an estate, so accuracy is essential.

Include brokerage and investment accounts, even if the balance is small. Every asset counts. For each account, record the brokerage name, the type of account, owner, and the present value: "John, personal brokerage account, Main Street Investments, $14,500." Also note life insurance policies, especially if they have a cash value. For policies like whole life or universal life, list the insurer, type of policy, name(s) of owner and insured, and cash value if any: "Lisa, whole life policy, Sunny Life Insurance, owner and insured, $12,000 cash value."

Real estate requires its grouping. Detail every property, even vacation cabins, rental homes, or empty land lots. State the address, description, approximate market value, and who owns it: "123 Maple Ave, primary residence, market value $400,000, owned jointly by John and Lisa." For timeshares or land parcels, mention the property type, company, and location: "Bear Valley Timeshare, Mountain Resorts, Lisa, $4,000 value."

Next, turn to vehicles. Count each car, truck, motorcycle, recreational vehicle, or boat, with model, year, and an estimated value: "John, 1968 Ford Mustang, classic car, individually owned, appraised at $10,000." Remember to include trailers, ATVs, and other vehicles if they have worth.

Round out assets with significant personal property. Think about jewelry, family heirlooms, antiques, collectibles, valuable electronics, musical instruments, artwork, or any special collections. Each item needs a brief description and estimated worth: "Lisa, diamond engagement ring, $2,500 estimated value." Grouping these things makes it easier to see where your most sentimental or valuable non-cash property lives.

Be as thorough and honest as possible. Missed items can cause disputes or confusion later. Even small retirement accounts or a piece of inherited jewelry should go on the list. If you're not sure of the value, use your best guess for now and adjust in the future.

After organizing your assets, move onto liabilities. Write down all debts and obligations still attached to you or shared with others. Start with home mortgages and lines of credit. For each, give the property address tied to the debt, name of lender, balance owed, and payment terms if you know them: "Home mortgage, 123 Maple Ave, National Home Lenders, $150,000 remaining, 30-year fixed, joint."

Car loans and other vehicle payments follow, each with the lender's name, vehicle description, amount owed, and loan term: "Car loan, 2019 Honda CR-V, Lisa, First Union Bank, $10,000 outstanding, five-year term." Don't forget student loans, medical bills, credit cards, and personal or business loans. Each entry should mirror the same level of detail: "Federal student loan, Lisa, $25,000 balance, U.S. Department of Education," "Credit card, John, Capital Plus, $2,500 balance, minimum due $60/month."

Group all debts together by type—real estate, auto, student, consumer credit—so you spot gaps or risks in your planning. This structure lays out both your obligations and the present strengths, making next steps easier.

Don't worry if values or balances aren't perfect. Write what you know, then update as you gather new information. The goal at this stage is to see your whole financial world at a glance. Having a well-sorted inventory means fast, smooth preparation for documentation.

Start gathering account statements, appraisals, and digital copies of titles or policies. These will support your records, make updates simple, and prove ownership and debts as you head deeper into estate planning.

Documenting Your Financial Information Clearly

Creating a thorough record-keeping system is one of the most valuable steps you can take after assembling your list of what you own and owe. Turning your inventory into an organized, easy-to-find record shifts it from a simple list to a tool that supports real protection and flexibility for yourself and your family. Well-documented records form the backbone of any estate plan. They remove confusion, prevent missed steps, and allow you and others to respond efficiently during yearly reviews or unexpected events.

Choosing your method of documentation depends on your comfort, privacy needs, and habits. People who prefer handwriting may use a dedicated notebook or a set of labeled folders. Digital users often choose spreadsheets, secure cloud documents, or estate planning software. Each format works as long as you commit to using it consistently and updating it as your life changes.

For each asset or debt, add accurate details that make your record truly useful. Start with the name of the item—for example, "ABC Bank Checking Account" or "Main Street Home Mortgage." Incorporate account or identification numbers, the full address of a property, or the VIN for a vehicle. Include who owns the asset—yours alone, shared with a spouse, or held in trust. Note how the account is titled, since this affects how the asset transfers. List the location of important papers, deed originals, or safe deposit keys.

Contact details are vital. Record the phone number or email for a bank, investment firm, or insurance company, along with a specific representative if possible. If an asset has an online login, document the username (avoiding passwords in open records) along with where and how login credentials are stored securely. When dealing with debts, list the lender's contact information, current terms, payment method, and the location of documents or online access points.

A repeatable structure makes the process simpler and helps you spot what is missing. Here's an approach for physical records:

- Use a set of folders divided by asset type (bank accounts, retirement, property, vehicles, life insurance, debts)
- Label each folder clearly with both content type and owner
- Place supporting documents (bank statements, deeds, titles, insurance certificates) in the correct folder
- Store the folders in a secure location like a locked drawer or safe

For digital records, mirror this system:

- Create a folder on your computer or a secure drive for each asset type
- Use consistent file names such as "2024 IRA Statement – ABC Investments" or "Car Loan Agreement – City Credit Union"
- Save digital scans or PDFs of physical records with clear descriptions
- Back up files on password-protected USB drives or secure cloud storage
- For extra assurance, keep a written guide or "map" of the folder system, indicating where key documents are saved and how to access them

A basic spreadsheet can become a powerful tool for tracking. List columns for asset type, account number, owner, institution, contact name, location of documents, date last checked, and special notes. Estate planning software often prompts for these details, and you can choose a program that fits your comfort with technology.

Regular review keeps your data accurate. Place a reminder in your calendar to check your inventory each year, as soon as you receive new account statements or after a big event like refinancing your mortgage or selling property. Use a checklist at the front of your documentation binder or digital folder to track the last update, who signed off, and when next to review. This habit prevents overlooked accounts or outdated addresses.

Here's a clear example of the difference organization makes:

Vague record: "Retirement accounts at XYZ Bank"

Actionable record:

- Asset: Roth IRA
- Institution: XYZ Bank
- Account number: 349021
- Owner: Joint (me and spouse)
- Branch contact: Andrea Lee, 555-9876
- Last statement location: Digital folder "Retirement/2024 Roth IRA"
- Online access: Username in password manager

Storing sensitive details safely matters as much as recording them. Never include passwords in plain view or unsecured files. For digital stores, use encrypted, password-protected documents and keep backup copies offline. Dedicated USB drives, locked file drawers, or secure home safes offer strong protection for physical documents.

Thorough documentation isn't just a personal shield; it's a gift to anyone who may need to act on your behalf someday. Detailed records save loved ones from confusion, delays, and stress during vital moments. Organizing now makes updates, sharing, and future transitions more manageable for all parties involved. Careful records pave the way for legal and family needs, ensuring all your work and planning truly count when they are most needed.

The Importance for Heirs and Legal Purposes

Putting together a detailed inventory of what you own and what you owe forms the backbone of any solid estate plan. Doing this helps your family and legal representatives avoid confusion or arguments later. When you leave behind a well-organized record of your finances, you save your heirs from long searches for missing documents, surprise debts, or heated debates over who should get what. For example, an updated list of your bank accounts, retirement plans, and real estate can turn a complicated legal process into a straightforward one. Your executor will have a clear roadmap to follow, letting them act quickly to pay off debts and distribute your property according to your wishes. Without this, your loved ones might spend months searching for accounts or struggle to pay final bills, all while dealing with grief.

Why Clear Inventories Make Things Easier

A full, up-to-date financial inventory isn't only for the wealthy. Every family, regardless of income or total assets, benefits from having this record. Imagine two siblings dealing with their parent's estate. If everything is spelled out on paper—even the details about an old car loan or a small insurance policy—there is less chance for resentment or suspicion. A clear inventory means no one needs to guess at your intentions or hunt for clues about what you owned. This reduces the risk of arguments or even legal contests.

Documentation can also protect against outside errors. Sometimes, banks freeze accounts because no one can immediately prove who should access them. If you leave behind a clear, legally accepted record that outlines your accounts, your executor can respond to questions with confidence and speed. This means your bills get paid on time, and your family isn't left waiting for funds they may urgently need for things like funeral costs or home expenses.

Legal Compliance and Avoiding Pitfalls

Estate laws require accurate reporting of all assets and debts. State and federal regulations often call for detailed lists that include property values, retirement accounts, cash, loans, and valuables such as jewelry or collectibles. Preparing these records in advance helps your executor save time and reduce legal costs, avoiding the need for professional asset searches. Some states even impose penalties on estates that fail to make timely or accurate disclosures, which can drain resources intended for your heirs.

If these requirements aren't met, the consequences can include expensive delays or, in serious cases, lawsuits. For example, if your plan omits several credit card debts and an overseas investment account, your executor might miss essential payments, resulting in added interest charges or legal claims against the estate. In addition, an incomplete or inaccurate inventory can give dissatisfied relatives grounds to challenge your will or dispute ownership of your assets. Courts may then freeze accounts or launch lengthy investigations, leaving your family in uncertainty until everything is resolved.

Peace of Mind for You and Your Loved Ones

Knowing that every detail is in place gives comfort both to you and to your loved ones. A thorough inventory becomes a living document. Life changes are easier to handle because you can update your record when you buy a new house, switch banks, split a retirement account in divorce, or change insurance beneficiaries. You're not stuck starting from scratch during a crisis or major life event.

Many people think listing their assets is too big a job or that only wealthy families benefit from these efforts. The truth is that families with modest means may face even greater challenges if there's confusion about bills or property. For example, if you leave a small life insurance policy but no one knows about it, your family may never claim the money you intended for them. Or, if you pass down a house but don't record unpaid property taxes, your heirs may inherit an unexpected cost.

Typical Assets and Liabilities to Include

Your inventory should cover:

Assets

- Checking and savings accounts
- Investment and retirement plans
- Real estate (homes, land)
- Vehicles
- Life insurance policies
- Personal property (valuables, jewelry, collectibles)

Liabilities

- Mortgages and home equity loans
- Credit card balances
- Car loans
- Personal loans

Including these means less chance your estate misses a payment or fails to secure a benefit. Bank accounts close properly, and old debts don't surprise heirs. Every step that you take to clarify these things now makes life easier for those you care about, lightening the emotional and practical burdens that can follow a loss. This sense of order and preparation gives you real peace of mind while offering clear support to those you may leave behind.

Bringing It All Together

Now that you clearly understand how to organize and document your assets and liabilities, you are ready to take the crucial next step in estate planning with confidence. By creating a detailed and well-maintained financial inventory, you lay the foundation for protecting your family's future, simplifying legal processes, and minimizing costs. This preparation not only reduces stress for your loved ones but also ensures your wishes are respected and followed smoothly when the time comes. Moving forward, keep your records updated regularly so that your estate plan remains accurate and effective, giving you peace of mind today and security for tomorrow.

CHAPTER 3
UNDERSTANDING WILLS – YOUR FIRST LINE OF CONTROL

More than half of adults in the United States pass away without leaving a valid will, leaving their families to face lengthy legal processes, unexpected expenses, and decisions made by courts rather than loved ones. When someone dies without clear instructions, state laws step in to divide property according to fixed rules that may not reflect personal wishes or family dynamics. Without this crucial document, even simple belongings can become sources of confusion and conflict among those left behind. Understanding how a will functions is the first step toward ensuring your intentions are honored, your assets protected, and your family shielded from unnecessary hardship.

What a Will Covers—and What Happens Without One

A will is a legal document that explains what should happen to your belongings after you pass away. If you own a house, a car, bank accounts, or items with personal meaning, your will specifies who should receive them. Many people imagine a will as something only the wealthy need, but in reality, it's useful for anyone who wants control over their home, cherished possessions, savings, or plans for their children's care.

A will applies to assets owned solely in your name. These might include a family home titled only to you, a car you purchased, your checking account, or a box of treasured letters stored in your attic. For example, if a parent owns a house and wants both children to inherit it equally, that wish can be stated clearly in the will. They might also leave jewelry to a sister or a vintage record collection to a close friend. All of this works only when the assets are owned by that individual alone and not shared with another person.

Some assets live outside a will's reach, regardless of what you write. Jointly owned assets, like a house co-owned with a spouse, skip the will entirely. These pass directly to the surviving owner by law. Retirement accounts, life insurance policies, and certain bank accounts have their own "beneficiary" forms. This means if you listed your nephew as your IRA beneficiary, even if your will says something else, that account will still go to your nephew. The same is true for property or accounts held in trust—you cannot change those directions with a will. These exceptions can surprise families who didn't realize the will's instructions only apply to certain types of property.

Let's look at a real-life example. Imagine Helen, a widowed mother, writes a will leaving her home to her daughter and her savings to her son. Her car, owned jointly with her son, does not appear in the will because it transfers to him directly. Her old life insurance policy, naming her friend as beneficiary, goes to the friend, even though the will states all assets go to her children. Because she only owned the family home in her name, her daughter receives it according to the will.

There are common misunderstandings about a will's powers. Some families guess a will can override beneficiary names on insurance or make changes to property already in trust, but it cannot. A will cannot direct who gets assets you have already promised elsewhere; it works only with property you own outright that doesn't have its instructions. Any plans involving family trusts, joint accounts, or designated insurance payments need separate legal work.

A will does not put conditions on how money is spent after you die unless you use specialized tools—like a trust within a will, which takes more legal steps. You cannot prevent someone from selling a house or mandate that the proceeds be spent in a specific manner using only an ordinary will. These situations require additional planning and should not rely solely on simple will language.

When a person dies without a valid will, their estate is considered "intestate." In this case, state inheritance laws take over and dictate who gets what. The court appoints an administrator—often the closest living relative—to manage everything. The result often surprises families. The process takes more time. There are extra court fees, plus the administrator has to account for every step, making things slower and sometimes more costly. The court divides property between close relatives in a set order, regardless of any emotional connections or verbal promises.

For example, when a mother dies without a will, her estate usually divides equally between her two adult children. But if she lived most of her life with a long-term partner, that person may receive nothing. If there are minor children, the court steps in and decides on a guardian, which may not be the person the parent wanted. Blended families face new problems: a stepchild raised as a daughter will not inherit unless named in a will. Unmarried partners, friends, or charities the person cared about all risk receiving nothing, since state law does not recognize informal promises or non-relatives.

These situations create hurt feelings, extra expenses, and sometimes long court fights. There is also a loss of privacy, since the probate process becomes a matter of public record. Family members might be left with a pile of paperwork just to claim the simplest things, like jewelry or household items.

To gain control and bring clarity, a person needs a legally valid will. That means putting wishes in writing, signing the document, and having witnesses watch and confirm the signing, as local law requires. Including every type of property, even digital or sentimental items, helps carry out the writer's true intentions. With this groundwork in place, anyone can begin to build a reliable will that protects their loved ones and reduces future uncertainty.

Steps to Writing a Legally Valid Will

Having a clear understanding of what a will can and cannot do prioritizes the next step: putting those wishes into writing in a manner recognized by the law. For your will to achieve its purpose after you pass away, every detail must line up with foundational legal standards. The foundation begins with comprehending the legal rules that provide a will with its validity.

Legal Requirements: Laying the Groundwork

A valid will starts with a testator, who must have the capacity to make one. Most places require the testator to be at least 18 years old. Mental capacity is just as critical. The law expects you to know the meaning of a will, be able to identify your property, and recognize the people you wish to benefit. Anyone struggling with serious confusion or under the control of someone else risks having their will thrown out.

Wills must be written, typed or handwritten. A will that is spoken out loud or written on a napkin does not count as valid. The document needs to show a "statement of testamentary intent," meaning it must plainly declare this is your will. "I declare this to be my Last Will and Testament" is a powerful sentence that makes a significant impact.

Witnesses and Signatures: Locking in Validity

Signing the will correctly is a central step. You, as the testator, must sign at the end of the will. If you can't sign, most places allow someone to sign for you in your presence and by your direction, but only if you're mentally able.

Witnesses are just as important as your signature. Most places require at least two, sometimes three, adults who don't stand to gain from your will. These witnesses must be "disinterested," meaning none can be an heir or beneficiary. Using a beneficiary as a witness is one of the most common blunders. Doing this can void gifts to that person or, in some cases, the entire will.

The process for witnessing usually looks like this:

1. Bring together your chosen witnesses.
2. Sign your will in front of them, or acknowledge a prior signature as your own.
3. Ask each witness to sign the will in your presence and in each other's presence.

Each jurisdiction has its quirks, but sticking to these broad points covers the basics.

Language and Clarity: Precision Over Guesswork

Wording is everything in a will. The best wills use clear, plain words to leave no room for different interpretations. If your will says, "I leave my personal items as my family needs," you risk sparking fights. The courts struggle to decide who counts as "family" and what you meant by "as my family needs." Better wording would be, "I leave my jewelry, listed on Schedule A, to my niece, Olivia Jones."

Here are some phrases that courts welcome:

- "I give my home at 123 Maple Lane, including all contents, to my son, Alex Lee."
- "My 2017 Toyota Camry goes to my daughter, Jasmine Doe."
- "My savings account at First City Bank, account number ending in 9287, will be divided equally between my grandchildren."

Problem phrases that spark family fights and court cases:

- "I leave my car to my child." (Which child? What if you have more than one?)
- "Divide my estate fairly." (What does "fairly" mean in dollars or items?)

Pay close attention to details that matter, such as names, addresses, or details about special items. The tighter the wording, the lower the chance of misunderstanding.

Respecting Jurisdictional Boundaries

One state's rule about witness numbers or signatures may not match another's. The steps above fit most places, but always double-check your local laws. You can do this by visiting your government's probate or courts website. Public law libraries or self-help centers have up-to-date guides you can use, and if you hit a snarl, a short meeting with a lawyer gives peace of mind your will is airtight.

Outlining Intentions: Keeping Everything Organized

Mapping out your wishes helps get your will from idea to finished document. Start with a worksheet or a list. Organize what you own and who should get each thing. Don't leave out digital accounts, computers, family photos, or collectibles. If you have pets or want to give something to charity, spell that out. If your child is young, name a guardian—and a backup. Keeping these sections organized prevents headaches for your loved ones.

For instance:

- House and land: Address, who gets it
- Vehicles: Make/model, recipient
- Personal belongings: Jewelry, art, digital assets
- Guardianship for children: Full names of guardians and alternates

Here's how clear plans matter. One family received a will that lumped "all precious things to my kids," but after the testator died, no one could agree what "precious" meant. The fight cost time and money. A neighbor of theirs listed his rare coin collection by year and left it to his niece. No disputes, no delays.

Outlining wishes also sets up the next vital step: choosing an executor. The executor will make sure every instruction you set out in your will happens as intended. Picking the right person for the job is the linchpin for these efforts, which deserves careful thought and planning.

Choosing an Executor: Selecting the Right Person for the Job

After writing out your wishes in a will, one key step remains between intention and reality: choosing the right person to carry them out. A will only works if someone trustworthy is responsible for the details once you're gone. This person is called the **executor**. They serve as the hands and voice of your wishes when you can no longer speak for yourself. The role goes far beyond a title—it determines how smoothly everything unfolds for the people you care about.

An executor's responsibilities extend well beyond sorting through keepsakes. Their first task is to gather information about everything you owned: bank accounts, property, investments, valuables, and debts. Identifying and valuing these assets often involves contacting banks, locating paperwork, and arranging professional appraisals. The executor is also responsible for paying what's owed, including outstanding bills and final taxes. They ensure loans, mortgages, and other debts are resolved, sometimes negotiating with creditors or closing accounts.

Only after these steps can the executor begin distributing what remains to the people named in your will. This might involve writing checks, transferring deeds, or closing accounts. Along the way, the executor works closely with banks, insurance companies, and occasionally the courts, which require official documentation and proof of action. Every step must follow your instructions precisely. The executor carries a legal duty to act fairly, transparently, and without any hint of personal benefit or conflict of interest.

Everyday dilemmas help show how this works. For example, if you owned a family house but still owed money on it, the executor might need to sell the house to pay off what you owed before passing anything on to your children. Sometimes a bank account is forgotten about and found only after searching through old records. These moments demand that the executor stay organized and patient.

A solid executor needs more than family ties. An individual who excels in managing paperwork, pays meticulous attention to detail, and maintains composure in stressful or emotional situations is the ideal choice. Honesty is a must, because people will be watching for fair action. Communication skills help too—relatives may have questions or concerns, and a clear, steady answer keeps mistrust from growing. Another overlooked factor is availability. Someone who lives nearby, who is not overwhelmed with other duties, and who can travel or make calls as needed is better suited than a loved one living across the country or overseas.

People often feel pressure to pick a spouse, eldest child, or close friend simply because of tradition or a personal bond. This sometimes leads to regret if the person is not skilled or available. Choose someone comfortable with financial matters and not afraid to ask for advice. Imagine choosing an executor who dreads paperwork and lets deadlines slip; this can cause missed tax filings, delays that frustrate your heirs, and even penalties. Family conflict is another real risk. For instance, making one child executor over others may trigger resentment, especially if your wishes are complicated or if the family is already divided.

Common pitfalls include picking someone who is absent-minded, overwhelmed, or too emotionally close to make objective choices. There are even cases where the wrong pick leads to endless arguments, the estate sits in limbo, and legal costs drain away much of what you hoped to leave behind.

Cautious decision-making helps prevent these issues. Before naming anyone as executor, have an honest conversation with them. Ask whether they are both willing and able to take on the work, given their own responsibilities and circumstances. In some estates, appointing two co-executors can help share the workload or balance different personalities, but this only works if both people cooperate and communicate effectively. In other cases, it can backfire when co-executors disagree, delaying the entire process. To prepare for the unexpected, name an alternate executor in your will in case your first choice cannot serve.

When it comes time to put this on paper, be precise. State the executor's full legal name and relationship to you. Write clearly: *"I appoint [Name] as the Executor of my will."* If you want two people to serve together, specify: *"I appoint [Name] and [Name] to act as Co-Executors."* Also include a backup plan: *"If [first choice] cannot serve, I appoint [alternate's name] as Executor."* Each instruction should be as clear as the directions used to describe your gifts and other provisions in your will.

By choosing carefully and communicating openly, you make the executor's difficult job manageable—and the aftermath of your passing far smoother for those you love. Preparation like this acts as a shield, protecting your family from confusion, conflict, and unnecessary costs when no will—or no reliable executor—is in place.

Bringing It All Together

Now that you understand the essential role a will plays in protecting your assets and ensuring your wishes are honored, it's time to take action by creating or updating your own. With clear, legally valid instructions and the right executor in place, you can reduce confusion, avoid costly legal battles, and provide peace of mind for yourself and your loved ones. Whether you own a home, care for children, or simply want to leave a thoughtful legacy, having a well-crafted will is a powerful step toward securing the future you envision. This clarity and preparation safeguard your property and lighten the burden on those you care about most when the time comes.

CHAPTER 4
LIVING TRUSTS – THE SECRET WEAPON TO AVOID PROBATE

"You won't have access to your money for months after a loved one dies." That chilling warning came from a friend who had just watched her family struggle through a drawn-out legal battle. She never imagined that settling an estate could be so slow, public, and costly—yet here she was, caught in the middle of court fees, waiting for approval, and worrying about how bills would get paid. Too many families face this reality every year because they didn't know there was another way. What if you could keep control while you're alive, protect your privacy, and, most importantly, spare those you care about from months of uncertainty? The solution lies in a tool many overlook or misunderstand—a living trust. It's not just legal paperwork; it's a carefully designed plan that can smooth the path when life takes unexpected turns. This chapter uncovers how living trusts work, their different forms, and why setting them up properly matters more than you might think.

The Essentials of Living Trusts and Major Types

A living trust is a legal document that lets a person, called the grantor, place their assets—like a house, bank accounts, or investments—under the care of another person, known as the trustee. The trustee manages these assets for the benefit of people that the grantor chooses, who are called beneficiaries. People use living trusts to manage what happens to their property after they pass away, but the benefits often go beyond this simple idea. Imagine a parent with young children who wants to make sure the family home is protected. They can set up a living trust so the house goes straight to their children if something happens to them. In another case, someone caring for an aging parent can put their savings and property in a trust to make sure bills get paid and financial needs are met.

Living trusts give people control while they are alive and offer peace of mind for what happens next. The main reason many families choose a living trust instead of just a will is to avoid probate. Probate is a court-managed process that happens after someone dies. It can be slow, public, and expensive. Probate often takes many months, and sometimes over a year, before loved ones receive what was meant for them. Big court fees and lawyer charges pile up. During this process, family members might wait months to access bank accounts that could help pay bills or manage everyday expenses.

People turn to living trusts because they keep matters private and move more smoothly. When assets are placed in a living trust, the trust—not the individual—owns those assets. After the grantor passes away, the trustee follows the instructions in the trust to transfer assets to beneficiaries. No court is needed to oversee this step, which means families can often take control more quickly. There's no long wait for the judge's approval, and no one outside the family needs to know what is happening. In many cases, this means a spouse or children can cover mortgage payments, medical bills, or other urgent needs without months of legal delays. Suppose a retired couple puts their home and savings into a living trust. If something happens, their children receive what they need to pay for a funeral, cover utility bills, and keep the house running right away.

Living trusts also offer more privacy. A will becomes a public record during probate, so anyone can see its contents. A living trust stays private, only shared with those who need to know. This gives families protection from nosy neighbors, prying relatives, or scammers scanning public court records. It's a quiet, respectful way to manage a family's legacy without putting every detail in front of the world.

Two main types of living trusts exist: revocable and irrevocable. Revocable trust is a flexible choice. The grantor keeps full control over the assets and the trust itself. They can change the trust's instructions, add or take out assets, or even cancel the whole thing at any time as long as they're alive and able. For example, imagine a working couple in their fifties who want to plan for their children's future, but they're not ready to make decisions that cannot be changed. By creating a revocable trust, they can add the family home and savings for now, knowing they can update or change things later if their family grows, they receive an inheritance, or their wishes change.

An irrevocable trust, on the other hand, is more strict. Once it's set up, the grantor cannot easily change or dissolve it. That may sound limiting, but the benefits matter for some families. The assets may be safe from lawsuits or creditors because the grantor no longer legally owns them. If a small business owner worries about legal claims against them, putting assets into an irrevocable trust can shield those assets from being taken in a lawsuit. Or, if a parent has health issues and wants to qualify for certain government benefits, transferring property to an irrevocable trust might help meet eligibility requirements.

Choosing between these trust types depends on how much control someone wants to keep, the risks they face, and their plans for the future. Skipping a trust entirely can lead to painful outcomes—long court battles, higher fees, and the risk that assets go to unintended people. Understanding the features of both revocable and irrevocable living trusts opens the door to smart estate planning that matches each family's values, goals, and needs. The path to choosing the right trust involves learning how each works and thinking carefully about what matters most for one's legacy and loved ones.

Comparing Revocable vs Irrevocable Trusts and Funding Your Trust

Choosing the right living trust means learning the practical trade-offs that can affect how you handle your own assets and protect your family. Living trusts come in two main types—revocable and irrevocable—and knowing the difference between them sets the stage for all the decisions that follow.

Revocable vs. Irrevocable: What Changes in Real Life

A revocable trust lets you stay in control. You can change the rules any time, add or remove property, or even end the trust if your needs shift. For example, a parent who wants to keep full say over a family home or investments while avoiding probate later will favor a revocable trust. This flexibility gives peace of mind but comes with certain limitations. Assets in a revocable trust remain yours for legal and tax purposes. If you owe debts, creditors can access the trust, and the assets are taxed as part of your estate.

Choosing an irrevocable trust means giving up more control—in exchange, you lock in powerful protections. Once set up, an irrevocable trust cannot be changed or dissolved unless the law or beneficiaries allow it. For someone facing looming legal claims or those looking to protect assets against nursing home costs, this can make sense. The moment you move property into an irrevocable trust, it no longer is yours directly. These assets are much more difficult for creditors to access, and depending on your state and timing, they might be exempt from estate taxes. Yet this loss of control is real: you can't take the assets back or change the terms easily. Choosing your type of trust is about lining up these pros and cons with your main goals.

Steps to Setting Up a Living Trust

The process of creating a living trust is clear and manageable when broken into actionable steps.

1. **Take stock of your assets**

Start by listing everything you wish to protect or pass on.

Homeowners often include their primary residence, a vacation cabin, or rental houses.

Families might write down checking and savings accounts, retirement plans, or investments such as stocks and bonds.

Collectors should not forget items with value, such as art, jewelry, or even vehicles.

2. **Choose between a revocable and irrevocable trust**

Your choice here shapes control, protection, and future options.

- If you want the ability to switch things up as life changes, a revocable trust keeps all doors open.
- If your main focus is shielding assets from lawsuits or government claims, then an irrevocable trust can provide that barrier, but you must be ready to hand over the reins for good.

3. **Pick your trustee**

The trustee manages the assets for the benefit of your chosen heirs.

Common picks include yourself (for revocable trusts), your spouse, or a dependable adult child. If your situation is more complex, you may want a professional or a trusted legal advisor. Always consider honesty, reliability, and an understanding of your wishes.

4. **Meet with an estate planning professional**

DIY trust forms exist, but laws differ between states. Legal missteps could cancel out your efforts. An expert helps craft documents that match your unique needs and are valid under local rules.

5. **Draft the trust document**

The trust spells out what assets will be managed, who benefits, and what happens under different circumstances. It should account for children, blended families, or key milestones, like when an heir turns eighteen.

6. **Sign and notarize the trust**

Formal signing by you and sometimes the trustee is required. Most states require a notary's stamp.

7. **Fund the trust: move assets into it**

This step makes the trust real. Each asset may need a different method:

- Real estate: Change the deed so the trust owns your home (ask at your county office for the proper forms).
- Bank accounts and investments: Change the account holder's name to the trust. Your bank will supply forms, or you can work with your advisor.
- Other valuables: Title cars, boats, or business shares in the trust's name if possible.

Why Funding Your Trust Matters

Failing to move property with the right paperwork can defeat your entire plan. A house left out of the trust must pass through probate, which adds cost and delay. Bank accounts not retitled stay outside the trust.

Keep a checklist. After funding, review your asset list once a year or after big life changes. Contact banks, investment offices, and government offices for proof that changes went through.

Looking Ahead

Setting up a living trust and putting assets into it is only part of the picture. Following the practical steps reduces risk, but pay attention to myths and common slip-ups that threaten your family's future. A little care now paves the way for smoother results and fewer surprises.

Common Misconceptions and Mistakes About Living Trusts

Every year, families hear promises that a living trust will guarantee a smooth transition after death, save money, and eliminate probate headaches. Advertisements call trusts "the magic bullet," and friends share stories of hassle-free inheritances. This confidence in living trusts stems from real advantages that both revocable and irrevocable trusts can offer. Trusts can bypass certain court procedures, provide control, and help organize your wishes. Yet many people fall for myths and make simple mistakes that lead to confusion, wasted time, and financial loss—right when their families need clarity the most.

The belief that creating a living trust completely eliminates probate is widespread. The appeal is obvious: probate sounds slow, expensive, and public. People long for a simple fix. However, a trust only avoids probate for assets that have actually been transferred into it. If your name still appears on a house deed or investment account, those assets remain outside the trust and must go through probate. A common scenario unfolds after someone's death: the family opens the trust expecting immediate access to property, only to discover the home or car was never retitled. The court intervenes, months pass, and legal fees drain the estate—exactly the outcome the trust was meant to avoid.

To prevent this, maintain an updated list of all assets and verify who holds official title. Double-check real estate deeds, vehicle registrations, stocks, bank accounts, and other major property. Many banks require special forms to transfer ownership. Keep written proof each time you add something to the trust. If your living trust doesn't legally "own" an asset, probate may still apply regardless of what the trust document states. Setting a yearly reminder to review property titles and account names provides an added layer of protection.

Another stubborn myth says that living trusts erase every tax. The idea comes from confusion about how trusts operate and a wish to escape estate or income taxes. Some families anticipate that a trust will reduce all taxes, including those on retirement funds and capital gains. The truth is, a revocable living trust does not remove assets from your taxable estate while you are alive because you still control everything inside. Irrevocable trusts function differently, but living trusts most often do not change your tax status.

The trap here results in unexpected bills. Take a family who puts their vacation home into a revocable trust, then sells it years later. Tax law still applies; capital gains tax comes due just as if they owned it directly. Consider an adult child who inherits a trust and believes there will be no taxes on those funds but then faces IRS penalties for misreporting. To steer clear, ask your attorney or financial advisor which taxes each trust affects. Never assume a trust automatically removes assets from all taxes. If saving on estate or income tax is the goal, you may need other solutions paired with your trust. Make a list of your goals up front, then have an expert walk through them line by line.

A subtle but dangerous mistake happens when people create trust but never fund it. This results from misunderstandings about how trust works in practice. Completing the paperwork makes the job feel like it's done. The trust folder sits on the shelf, but nothing ever moves into its name. Years later, loved ones discover a beautifully written trust that holds nothing, and all the property ends up in probate. The solution is concrete: after signing the trust, gather all ownership documents and follow through with each transfer. Some accounts take minutes at a branch; others, like real estate, need an updated deed filed with the county. Use a checklist, then verify every transfer with bank statements or title documents before storing your trust paperwork.

Neglecting ongoing trustee duties and updates rounds out the list of costly errors. Life is full of changes: marriage, divorce, new children, a new home, or a falling out with a relative. Many believe once they write their wishes into the trust, those choices will always reflect their true intentions. Over time, an outdated trust may leave assets to people no longer in the family, skip a new grandchild, or fail to meet current laws. Old beneficiaries can end up with property that you intended for others. To prevent this, plan to review your trust every two to three years or after big life events. Update your asset schedule and any new accounts. Write down dates of revisions, and make sure everyone who needs the new version gets it.

People often believe that living trusts will fix everything once they sign the documents. In practice, much depends on careful titling, regular updates, and honest checks on facts and goals. A little extra attention now can spare your loved ones confusion and cost later.

Bringing It All Together

Now that you understand the key features, types, and steps involved in setting up a living trust, you are better equipped to take control of your estate plan and protect your family's future. By carefully choosing between revocable and irrevocable trusts, properly funding your trust, and avoiding common mistakes, you can ensure your assets transfer smoothly, privately, and with fewer costs. This knowledge empowers you to make informed decisions that align with your goals and values, giving you confidence that your loved ones will be cared for without unnecessary legal hurdles or delays. Taking action now sets the foundation for a secure legacy and peace of mind for years to come.

CHAPTER 5
APPOINTING KEY PEOPLE – EXECUTORS, GUARDIANS, AND POWER OF ATTORNEY

More than half of all estate plans run into complications because the right people were not chosen or thoroughly prepared to step into key roles when needed. Executors, guardians, and agents with power of attorney hold responsibilities that can shape how smoothly a family weathers difficult times. Selecting individuals for these roles is not just about trust; it requires careful thought about their ability to manage complex tasks, communicate and handle sensitive situations. Without clear conversations and well-defined expectations, even the most thoughtfully prepared plans can lead to confusion, delays, and conflict. This chapter offers guidance to help you make informed choices and ensure those entrusted with your affairs are ready to act with confidence and care.

Selecting the Right Executor and Communicating Expectations

Almost every estate plan depends on selecting someone willing and capable of serving as executor. This person steps in after your death to ensure that the wishes in your will are carried out. The executor gathers assets, pays debts and taxes, manages accounts, files paperwork with the court, ensures bills are settled, and distributes what remains to the people or organizations you've named. For many families, the executor also serves as a bridge between the legal process and those awaiting their inheritance. It's more than just completing paperwork; it's about guiding others through a difficult time with respect and fairness. When choosing an executor, most people think of a trusted family member or friend, though some opt for a lawyer or professional fiduciary for additional support.

Here are the main tasks every executor must handle:

- Collecting financial documents and locating assets like homes, vehicles, investments, and valuables
- Notifying banks, utility companies, government offices, and other involved parties
- Paying outstanding bills, credit cards, mortgages, and taxes
- Keeping clear records of all income and expenses tied to the estate
- Working with the probate court to meet all legal filing deadlines
- Communicating with beneficiaries to let them know where things stand and what comes next
- Distributing assets according to the will only after debts and taxes are settled

Naming just one person as executor can leave an estate plan vulnerable if that person is suddenly unable or unwilling to serve. Life circumstances can change. A chosen executor might move far away, fall ill, decide the responsibility is too much, or even pass away first. Sometimes family relationships take an unexpected turn, and someone once named might not be the right fit later. That is why almost every solid estate plan names a backup—or alternate—executor. The backup steps in if the first person cannot or will not act. Imagine an estate where the only named executor declines the role or becomes unreachable. The family could be left with delays, disputes, or even a judge deciding who takes over. Listing a backup helps avoid extra paperwork and confusion at one of the worst possible times.

Some people ask a close sibling to be their main executor and a trusted longtime friend as backup. Others prefer a mix, such as naming a family member first and a professional second. The most important thing is that everyone named is comfortable with the job and has the right qualities.

When searching for the right executor, focus on trustworthiness and proven reliability. This person must deal with sensitive information and follow instructions exactly. A solid executor notices details, meets deadlines, and stays organized even when under pressure. The best choice is to be open and calm in communicating with others, especially when people are grieving. Fairness helps prevent hurt feelings or arguments among family. Someone who can manage paperwork and take care of practical tasks, from closing accounts to talking to lawyers, will find the job easier. If a brother and sister don't see eye-to-eye or have quarreled for years, neither makes a good executor if the will's beneficiaries include both. Strong emotions or family drama can stall the entire process.

There are a few legal rules. In most states, an executor must be at least 18 years old and not currently in legal trouble. A "felon" is often barred from serving. Some states require the executor to live in the same state as the person whose estate they are handling, or, if they don't, to appoint a state resident as a representative. Laws can change, so readers should always double-check with a local attorney or look up their state's requirements if they suspect their situation might not be typical.

Raising the question with a possible executor often makes people nervous, but being open from the start helps everyone. Respect matters. Pick a relaxed setting and explain what the role involves in plain terms—handling money, making decisions, and dealing with paperwork. Emphasize why you trust them and give them a chance to voice hesitations or ask questions. Bringing copies of your will and a list of important document locations demonstrates trust. Let them know how they might get help from attorneys or accountants, and make sure they understand they don't have to accept the job right away.

Clarity prevents problems. If an executor knows what to expect and agrees to serve, things move forward more smoothly. But when someone is asked only after the death, they may feel confused or pressured. Some families have faced legal delays because an executor refused the job or struggled to find key paperwork. Others have watched old resentments flare up and slow everything down when a loved one never explained their choice. Simple conversations now save complications later.

Choosing responsible people for critical roles starts with the executor, but it doesn't end there. For families with minor children, deciding who will step in as guardian is just as important—asking different questions, but with the same goal: keeping loved ones safe and supported when they need it most.

Appointing Guardians for Minor Children and Having Essential Conversations

Taking steps to choose the right guardian for minor children comes from the same sense of responsibility that guides the choice of an executor. While executors safeguard your assets and wishes, guardians protect your children's growth, health, and security. Where an executor manages paperwork and financial tasks, a guardian's responsibility extends every day—providing care, emotional support, and stable guidance. Children need not just shelter and education but someone devoted to keeping family routines, beliefs, and connections alive.

A guardian steps in if both parents become unable to provide care. This includes everything from getting children to school and doctor appointments to celebrating birthdays in ways that feel familiar. Over the long term, the guardian might steer big decisions: what community they live in, how faith or family traditions are honored, and how relationships with relatives and friends continue. Occasionally a guardianship is short if a parent recovers from illness or injury, but often it covers the rest of the child's youth. The person you choose will have a daily role in shaping everything from your child's confidence to their sense of belonging.

Evaluating Potential Guardians

A strong choice for a guardian is built on more than trust. One practical way to start: make a list of everyone you consider and weigh each candidate against a set of factors, such as

- **Willingness and comfort with the role:** Begin by thinking, "Would this person want to do this?" Some people might feel honored; others may be uneasy or too burdened. Ask yourself, "Can I picture them thriving in this responsibility, or might they struggle?"
- **Beliefs and values:** Does the candidate have views on parenting, discipline, religion, and education that match yours? For example, if you value open communication or regular gatherings with extended family, will the guardian continue those traditions? Imagine a guardian who is patient and nurturing for a sensitive child; that kind of match smooths the transition if the day comes.
- **Parenting style:** Consider how the guardian manages their own children or interacts with others. If a possible guardian is very strict but you use gentle guidance, there may be friction. Observing how this person responds to everyday stresses—bedtime battles, school issues—offers clues about future success.
- **Family dynamics and existing relationships:** Sometimes the "obvious" person may not suit the child's needs. Suppose a close relative tends to tension with your child, while a good friend steps in as a positive influence. Ask, "Is the bond supportive, or would it add new stress?"

- **Financial stability and resources:** While guardians needn't be wealthy, they should be able to provide for basic needs without strain. Your estate can support guardians financially, but a baseline of stability opens more options for the child's experiences and education.
- **Personal health and geographic location:** A thriving guardian invests energy, time, and care. Consider the person's health, age, and living situation. If you want your child to stay in a certain city or near school friends, location matters.
- **Openness to ongoing connection:** The right guardian is not only willing but also able to keep your child linked to extended family, community, and cultural roots.

Approaching the Conversation

When you identify likely choices, prepare for a conversation grounded in respect and care. Start simply. Share why you are considering them and what values guide your choice. Outline basic expectations, such as where the child might live, day-to-day routine details, and hopes for education or religious upbringing. Encourage honest questions and concerns. Simple language works best:

- "We'd like you to consider taking this role if something happens to us, and we want to talk through what it might look like."
- "Your views about raising kids are close to ours, and we see you as someone who could help them feel safe and loved."

Give the person time to reflect before deciding. Invite their candid thoughts about readiness or reservations. If they feel hesitant, honor that feeling and affirm your trust regardless of the outcome. If there are differing opinions in the family or a strained connection between child and guardian, name it openly and discuss goals: "We value peace and want to avoid tension, but we also believe ___ offers the stability our child would need." Listen for feedback, and where needed, consult a neutral adviser for perspective.

Keeping Plans Clear and Current

Once a guardian agrees, keep the conversation active. Review plans every couple of years or after significant changes—like moving, health issues, or shifts in family structure. Use a letter of wishes, written in plain language, to highlight routines, traditions, bedtime stories, annual trips, or guiding values you hope will stay constant. Deliver this letter with warmth and openness, promising an ongoing dialogue so that no one faces surprises. A thoughtful choice, careful discussion, and shared understanding lay the best foundation for the rest of your planning.

Understanding Powers of Attorney and Discussing Roles with Chosen Agents

Some choices in estate planning need more than just careful thought —they also demand taking action before a crisis. A power of attorney, or POA, stands as one of those legal tools that lets someone else act in your place if you cannot manage things yourself. These documents allow another person—the agent—to step in and handle business or health matters when you are unable to do so. Having both a medical power of attorney and a financial power of attorney in place gives you control over who handles your care, money, and daily affairs at the moments that matter most.

Medical and financial powers of attorney work for separate but vital parts of life. The medical power of attorney allows the agent to make healthcare decisions if illness or injury leaves you unable to speak for yourself. For example, your agent may have to say yes or no to a proposed surgery, discuss treatment plans with doctors, or guide end-of-life care according to your wishes. Nearby hospitals or physicians often require a clear authorization to allow someone else to decide for you. Without a valid medical POA, uncertainty and delay can get in the way of fast treatment.

A financial power of attorney, on the other hand, deals with money and property. Your agent may need to pay bills, manage bank accounts, sign checks, handle insurance matters, or even sell a house while you recover from illness or injury. Real-world situations call for the agent to act while you're in the hospital, in rehab, or facing any situation where you cannot sign a legal document yourself. Having the financial POA in place helps ensure the mortgage gets paid, utilities stay on, and assets remain safe.

Distinctions Between Medical and Financial Powers

Medical and financial POAs may sound similar, but they come with different boundaries and responsibilities. A medical POA does not give the agent access to your bank accounts, just as a financial POA does not let the agent decide about surgeries or medications. Some people choose the same person for both roles, but it's important to match the right person to each set of duties. Communication preferences, personal trust, and availability also factor into these choices.

When Both Are Needed

Imagine an older adult in the hospital after a car accident. A medical POA agent works with doctors to approve surgery and monitor medications, while a financial POA agent handles rent, insurance, and other pressing bills. If both agents do their jobs well, recovery can happen without outside stress or confusion. Skipping one piece often means someone's needs—health or financial—could be overlooked.

Key Qualities for POA Agents

Medical POA agents do best when they can stay calm in emergencies. They need to listen to your wishes, respect your beliefs, and handle tough conversations with healthcare providers. Strong communication helps—so does the ability to speak up under pressure. Being nearby can also make things smoother, as medical decisions often require quick action.

Good financial POA agents need solid money sense. They should be organized, trustworthy, and careful with paperwork. Someone who can stay on top of due dates, keep records, and keep their money separate from yours brings peace of mind. For more complicated estates, someone with an understanding of accounts or investments can be a plus. Some look for a backup—or contingent—agent, naming a second person in case the first cannot serve. This extra step keeps your affairs on track no matter what.

Starting Hard but Honest Conversations

Bringing up these roles can feel awkward, but clear talk saves families from second-guessing later. Try these steps to start the conversation:

- Choose a private, low-stress time to talk.
- Explain why you trust this person for the role: "You've always managed your money carefully, and I want someone level-headed looking out for me."
- Lay out the duty: "This doesn't mean I'm expecting a crisis soon, but I want to be ready."
- Ask if they're comfortable and willing, without pressure.

Use open-ended prompts to guide dialogue:

- "How do you feel about making healthcare choices if I can't speak for myself?"
- "Are you open to stepping in if my finances need daily attention due to illness?"
- "What concerns or questions come to mind about either responsibility?"
- "Would you rather be a backup in case my first choice is unavailable?"

Formalizing Arrangements and Avoiding Conflict

After an honest agreement, get everything in writing. Share the legal documents with your chosen agents and any professionals (like doctors or banks) who may need them. Keep signed copies in an accessible, safe place. Let other family members know your decisions in advance, to head off misunderstandings.

Check back every so often: health, relationships, and trust can all change. Keeping documents and instructions up-to-date, along with ongoing talks, builds the foundation for smooth support if life takes a sudden turn. Early, open planning steers everyone through hard moments with less confusion and more confidence.

Bringing It All Together

Now that you understand how vital it is to choose the right people for key roles in your estate plan—and to communicate their responsibilities clearly—you can take confident steps to protect your family's future. By carefully selecting trustworthy executors, guardians, and agents for powers of attorney who are prepared and willing to serve, you reduce the risk of confusion, delays, or disputes when it matters most. Open conversations and regular updates ensure everyone involved knows what to expect and can act smoothly when called upon. With these tools and thoughtful choices in place, you can move forward knowing your wishes will be honored, your loved ones supported, and your estate handled with care and respect.

CHAPTER 6
MEDICAL DIRECTIVES AND END-OF-LIFE PLANNING

When faced with serious illness or unexpected medical emergencies, having clear instructions about your healthcare wishes becomes essential. Many people avoid thinking about these situations until they arise, but without preparation, decisions can become confusing and stressful for both patients and their families. Knowing how to communicate your preferences in advance protects your rights and provides peace of mind, ensuring that your values guide the care you receive even when you cannot speak for yourself.

This chapter will explore how to formalize your healthcare decisions through important legal documents such as living wills, advance directives, and Do Not Resuscitate (DNR) orders. It will explain how these tools work together to make your wishes known and respected. You will also learn about the role of organ donation preferences in end-of-life planning and practical steps to create, finalize, and store these documents properly. By understanding these elements, you can take control of your medical future and help secure the well-being of your loved ones.

Living Wills, Advance Directives, and DNR Orders: Formalizing Your Healthcare Decisions

Serious medical decisions can arrive with little warning. When a person cannot speak for themselves, having clear instructions in place helps avoid confusion and protects the right to choose the type of care received. Medical directives are written legal documents that spell out these wishes. There are several kinds that work together: living wills, advance directives, and Do Not Resuscitate (DNR) orders. Each serves a different role, but all share the goal of making sure a person's preferences are honored in moments when it matters most.

A **living will** is a document that explains what kinds of medical treatment a person does or does not want if they become unable to communicate, often due to serious illness or injury. For example, a living will may state whether a person wants life-prolonging treatments such as a feeding tube, mechanical ventilation, or dialysis if they are in a coma or a persistent vegetative state. Some include preferences for pain management, even if it could shorten life, or instructions to avoid certain procedures entirely. The document only takes effect once doctors determine that the person cannot make decisions on their own.

Many families have endured long, stressful hospital stays when loved ones had no written guidance. Disagreements can easily arise among siblings or spouses about what a parent would have wanted, with no clear answer. But when a properly signed living will is in place, the family and care team know exactly how to proceed.

Advance directives are broader legal instructions that can include a living will but often go further. In most states, an advance directive lets you appoint a trusted person—a health care proxy, agent, or medical power of attorney—who can legally make health decisions on your behalf if you cannot. These instructions can outline what treatments are acceptable, who may be involved in decisions, and which hospitals or doctors you prefer.

Advance directives are especially valuable in cases of sudden incapacity, such as a stroke or major accident, as well as during long-term illness. For example, imagine a teacher who names his son as his agent in an advance directive. When he unexpectedly collapses and is hospitalized, doctors know to turn to his son for decisions rather than leaving the family uncertain or waiting for a court to intervene. Missing or unclear directives can lead to unwanted tests, prolonged treatments the person never would have chosen, or lasting regret among family members.

A Do Not Resuscitate order (DNR) addresses a single decision: whether to use cardiopulmonary resuscitation (CPR) if a person's heart or breathing stops. This document is often completed in hospitals, nursing homes, or with the help of a doctor for people with advanced illness. For many, a DNR brings comfort by signaling a desire for a natural death, wishing to avoid medical interventions that can be painful or unlikely to work. Others may decide against a DNR, wanting every attempt at revival regardless of their condition. A DNR must be clear and present in the patient's file or posted in the care facility; otherwise, EMS or doctors usually provide full resuscitation by law.

Some people believe that having a **living will** means they don't need an **advance directive**, or that a **Do Not Resuscitate (DNR)** order makes the other documents unnecessary. These are common misunderstandings. A living will records treatment preferences but may not cover every situation or unexpected event. An advance directive adds a trusted decision-maker and additional instructions, offering broader protection. A DNR applies only to CPR decisions and doesn't address other care, such as comfort measures or feeding tubes. Each document complements the others, creating a detailed and flexible plan that reflects a person's values and needs.

Common questions often arise. *"Can I change these documents later?"* Yes. Medical directives can be updated or revoked at any time, as long as you're able to make your own decisions. *"What if my family disagrees with my wishes?"* As long as the documents meet state legal standards, health care providers are required to follow them even if family members object. *"What if my medical situation isn't covered?"* Naming a health care agent through an advance directive ensures that your preferences are represented by someone who knows you well.

Lives are made easier when people take the time to create and update these directives. Families avoid unnecessary heartache, and patients receive care that truly matches their wishes. This is part of a broader process—careful, thoughtful planning for the end of life. Alongside medical choices, it can also include reflecting on your legacy and considering the meaningful act of organ or tissue donation.

Organ Donation Preferences: Making Your Wishes Known

Taking charge of your medical decisions starts with spelling out treatment preferences, but the same sense of control also lets you make choices about organ and tissue donation. When you include organ donation in your planning, you shape what happens to your body in a way that can help others and keep your beliefs front and center. This extends your ability to direct your care and legacy, even in moments when decisions happen quickly and you cannot speak for yourself.

What Organ and Tissue Donation Means

Organ donation means giving permission for doctors to remove organs or tissues from your body after death, usually to save someone else's life or improve their health. Commonly donated organs include the heart, lungs, kidneys, liver, pancreas, and intestines. Tissues such as corneas, skin, bone, heart valves, and tendons also help people. For example, a single donor's organs can help up to eight different people. Tissue donation may allow someone blinded by injury to see again or help a burn victim heal and regain mobility. Donated organs and tissue can give families waiting for transplants hope in accidents that claim lives.

For organ donation to happen, you usually need to pass away in a hospital while on life support, because the organs must be kept healthy until they are recovered. Tissue donation has broader circumstances, since many tissues stay useful for hours even after the heart stops. Both forms offer a final act of care, turning tragedy into new chances for others.

Range of Choices

You can decide to:

- Donate all organs and tissues allowed by law.
- Donate only certain organs or tissues you choose, such as kidneys or corneas.
- Decline all organ or tissue donation.

Some people want to set limits based on their beliefs, family history, or views about illness and death. For instance, a person might feel comfortable donating their corneas but not their heart. Others only want to donate if doctors determine their body can help in a meaningful way. All of these choices are valid and respected when they are clear.

Values, Beliefs, and Traditions

Religious and cultural beliefs play a strong role in donation decisions. Some faiths view organ donation as a final act of charity, such as many Christian and Jewish traditions that encourage helping others, while some Muslim leaders support giving as long as it does not harm the body unnecessarily. Other groups may discourage it, either because of rules about burial or beliefs about the body after death. Sometimes, misunderstandings or stories within a family also guide views. For example, one family may uphold a tradition of giving, while another values keeping the body whole. You do not have to follow any example but your conviction. You can seek advice from your faith leader or a trusted elder if you wish.

How to Register and Document Your Wishes

Registering your decision is easy and gives it the power of law in most states. Most people sign up through their state's Department of Motor Vehicles (DMV), which adds a tag or symbol to your driver's license. You can also join your state's or a national donor registry online or by phone. These steps connect your preferences to the official records that doctors consult during an emergency. Still, listing your wishes in your medical directive or living will keep your decisions tied to your other care instructions. Add clear statements like "I wish to donate my organs and tissues," or list only those you are willing to give.

Many think doctors ignore care if you are an organ donor, but this is false. Doctors who treat you in an emergency work to save your life, no matter your donor status. Only after death does the organ recovery team review your registration. People with cancer, diabetes, or other illnesses can still donate some tissues or organs, depending on their condition. Never decide based on old myths. Always ask your doctor if you have questions about your health and donation.

Talking With Loved Ones

Making a donation can feel personal and emotional. Still, it helps avoid confusion and conflict later if everyone hears your wishes from you directly. Use stories to show why the choice matters. For instance, you might talk about a neighbor who received a heart transplant or how your own family values giving. Invite questions and give time for feelings to surface. Sometimes, writing a short note or recording a message supports your plan. People involved in your care—such as your healthcare proxy, adult children, or close friends—should understand and agree to honor your decision.

Next Steps for Complete Clarity

Organ donation is one part of the bigger picture. Recording this choice points the way to writing down all your end-of-life care wishes and keeping your directives safe and accessible. Just as conversations about donation protect your intent, honest, careful documentation will safeguard every important medical choice when the time comes.

Creating, Finalizing, and Storing Medical Directives: Practical Implementation Steps

Clear and open communication about organ donation is a meaningful act for both you and your family. By deciding and documenting your intentions, you protect loved ones from the stress of having to guess or disagree during a high-pressure moment. All medical directives share this basic purpose—making your choices known, reducing confusion, and ensuring your voice is heard when you might otherwise be silent.

Keeping your medical wishes confined to conversations is not enough. Documents like a living will, an advance directive, a Do Not Resuscitate (DNR) order, and an organ donation statement should exist in forms that doctors and hospitals can legally follow. Each directive covers a unique part of your care:

- **Living Will:** States what types of life-sustaining treatments you want—or don't want—if you become unable to communicate, such as feeding tubes, breathing machines, or CPR.
- **Advance Directive:** Covers a broader scope than a living will, allowing you to select a trusted person (a healthcare proxy or agent) who will make medical decisions for you if you are unable.

- **DNR Order:** Tells health professionals you do not want attempts at resuscitation if your heart or breathing stops. This must be a formal, signed medical document recognized by hospitals and emergency responders.
- **Organ Donation Statement/Card:** Expresses your wish to donate organs or tissue after death. This can appear on your driver's license, a standalone card, or a written statement.

Getting these forms is simple. Start with your state's health department website or ask your doctor's office. Hospitals often provide them for free. Reputable nonprofit organizations online, like the National Hospice and Palliative Care Organization or state bar associations, offer downloadable versions. Always use the version valid in your state—small details can differ.

You usually need to be an adult, and some states require that you are of sound mind when signing. Read each form closely. Be sure to fill in every section thoroughly, choosing clear, plain answers to questions about treatments or your choice of decision-maker. Never leave blanks—gaps may cause confusion or invalidate the document. For the living will, spell out unexpected details. For example, if you wish to refuse a feeding tube but still want comfort care, specify that.

For your directives to stand up in an emergency or legal setting, follow your state's full requirements about signing, witnessing, and notarizing. Most forms must be signed by you and witnessed by one or two adults. These people should not be named as your agent, heirs, or doctor—pick witnesses with no "stake." Some states require a notary stamp. As you sign, double-check that all boxes are filled, names are spelled right, and the right people are present.

Missing a witness or using the wrong form can undo all your planning. Imagine a person signs a living will and thinks it is valid, but both witnesses are family heirs. In a crisis, doctors may set aside the document because state law forbids heirs from witnessing. The result: your medical decisions could go against your wishes. To avoid this, ask a nurse, social worker, friend, or neighbor who is not included in your will to witness. Review every page against state requirements before considering it done.

Where and how you keep these papers matters. Store original documents in a fireproof home safe or a locked file, rather than in a hard-to-access safety deposit box. Give signed copies to your main doctor, designated healthcare agent, and local hospital for their files. Some people upload digital scans to a secure online health portal or emergency document service. It helps if you carry a simple wallet card stating you have advance directives, with clear contact information for your healthcare agent or the location of your documents.

Share your signed directives with everyone who needs to know: doctors, the person you named as your decision-maker, and close family. Do not assume they will always know where to look. Using digital registries—either provided by your state or a major healthcare system—can ensure hospital staff access your forms in a crisis.

Review your directives every few years, or after major changes like marriage, divorce, a new diagnosis, or moving. Check with your healthcare agent that they are still able and willing to honor your wishes. To start a conversation, you might say, "I want to talk about my wishes for medical care if I can't speak for myself. There are forms I filled out, and here's what they mean." Or with doctors: "I have an advance directive and living will. Let's make sure you have them on file."

Simple, well-prepared documents, shared with those who count, save loved ones from stress and uncertainty—and make sure your choices are honored.

Concluding Thoughts

Now that you understand the importance and distinct roles of living wills, advance directives, DNR orders, and organ donation statements, you can take confident steps to formalize your healthcare decisions. By creating, updating, and securely storing these documents, and by sharing them clearly with those who matter most, you protect your wishes from confusion or dispute when you cannot speak for yourself. This proactive planning safeguards your rights and eases the burden on loved ones during difficult times. Moving forward, make it a priority to review your directives regularly and communicate openly, ensuring your medical care and legacy reflect your values and choices with clarity and respect.

CHAPTER 7

MINIMIZING TAXES AND LEGAL COSTS

Many people believe estate planning is simply about deciding who inherits their belongings, but the reality is far more complex—and costly. If you don't carefully consider taxes and legal fees, you risk losing a significant portion of your assets before they reach your loved ones. This chapter challenges the assumption that estate planning is only for the wealthy and reveals how strategic steps can help families of all sizes protect what matters most.

This chapter explores practical ways to minimize the impact of estate taxes and reduce legal expenses through thoughtful planning. It guides you through understanding key tax concepts, using trusts effectively, managing legal costs, and integrating life insurance into your plan. By focusing on these areas, you can safeguard your family's financial future while avoiding unnecessary burdens and fees.

Understanding Estate Taxes and Tax-Saving Tools

Estate planning isn't only about deciding who gets what—it's about making sure more of what you own actually reaches the people you care about. For most adults managing their homes, savings, and retirement accounts, keeping more of their assets in the family often means learning the basics of taxes and costs that come with handling an estate. Knowing how taxes work and the smart moves you can make will help you avoid surprises, fight off extra expenses, and give your family the peace of mind they deserve.

Estate taxes rarely apply to most families, but understanding them gives you a sense of control. An estate tax is a tax on your total assets at death, before they go to heirs. This is different from an inheritance tax, which some states charge when someone actually receives money or property, and different again from the gift tax, which is triggered if you give away too much in a single year or over your lifetime. The federal estate tax only applies to estates valued over $12.92 million as of 2023. That number means most Americans won't pay a federal estate tax at all. For example, if your total assets—such as your house, retirement accounts, cars, investments, and even personal items—add up to under $12.92 million when you die, the federal government will not take a portion through estate tax.

Some states set their estate tax rules, and their thresholds are often much lower than the federal level. For instance, Massachusetts and Oregon impose estate taxes that begin on estates valued between $1 million and $2 million. If you live in or own property within one of these states, it's important to understand both state and federal regulations to see whether your assets could be affected. Even if the federal threshold seems far off, the value of your home or life insurance could push your total assets higher—especially in high-cost areas or after years of appreciation.

Consider two common examples. The first is a couple in their sixties who own a home valued at $450,000, have $300,000 in retirement savings, and have around $50,000 in other investments and cash. Their total estate, at roughly $800,000, falls well below the $12.92 million federal limit, so they won't owe federal estate taxes. Unless they live in a state with a lower threshold, estate taxes are unlikely to affect their plan.

The second example involves a family that owns a business, several investment properties, and homes in two different states worth about $8 million, along with retirement and investment accounts. Their total estate approaches—or exceeds—both federal and state limits. Without proper planning or professional guidance, a significant portion of their wealth could go to taxes instead of their heirs. Families who receive large inheritances, build successful businesses, or hold substantial life insurance policies can sometimes find their estates growing into taxable territory without realizing it.

Small actions now can keep more assets in your family's hands. One of the strongest ways to lower possible estate taxes is creating a trust. A trust is a legal arrangement where you transfer assets to a trustee, who then manages those assets for your chosen beneficiaries (like children). Trusts come in different types. A revocable living trust lets you keep control and change things if needed, but the assets still count toward your estate's value for tax purposes. An irrevocable trust means giving up control—you can't simply take things back—but the assets placed inside do not count toward your taxable estate anymore. A family with a high-value life insurance policy may place it in an irrevocable trust, removing the payout value from their taxable estate and handing it more cleanly to children.

Some parents create a special needs trust for a child, both to provide for lifelong care and to keep those funds separate from taxes or limits that apply to direct assets. Charitable trusts help by donating to a cause, letting you lower the taxable amount and support something you believe in at the same time.

Giving gifts during your life is another way to lower estate taxes. The IRS allows you to give up to $17,000 to someone in 2023 without paying gift tax or reducing your lifetime exemption. That means a couple could give $17,000 each to each of their children, every year, passing down wealth and reducing the value of their estate for tax purposes. If your estate may grow near the limit, giving some away early can make a meaningful difference.

Tax-advantaged accounts help on another front. IRAs, 401(k)s, and 529 college savings plans all allow you to name a beneficiary. When you do this, those assets can pass directly to your chosen person without going through probate, sometimes skipping state estate tax or lowering exposure. For example, naming your spouse as the beneficiary on your IRA lets those funds go straight to them; no court involvement is needed. Taxes on certain account withdrawals still apply, but naming beneficiaries avoids delays and legal fees connected to probate.

Taxes are not the only factor that can eat up your family's legacy. Legal costs and fees can shrink an estate if planning is ignored or done in a hurry. Paying attention to both taxes and fees is step one in building an estate plan that truly protects your family's wellbeing and wealth for the long run.

Managing and Reducing Legal Costs

Families often hear about estate tax planning, but costs can also mount from the legal side if not carefully managed. Protecting assets and ensuring wishes are honored means understanding not only where legal bills lurk but also how to cut them down to size. Care in this area lets more of your assets go to loved ones, easing their burden when the time comes.

Types of Legal Costs in Estate Planning

Legal expenses in estate planning come in several forms. Some are upfront and easy to see, while others hide in the details and unexpected events.

- **Attorney fees** stand out as the most visible cost. These may be:
  - **Hourly**: The lawyer charges for each hour spent on your matter. Complex families or several rounds of revisions make this cost rise fast.

  - **Flat fees**: For set services, like simple wills or power of attorney documents, the lawyer quotes a price before work starts.
  - **Percentages**: Sometimes, for managing estates through probate, lawyers may charge a percentage of the total estate value, which can add up when assets are high.
- **Court filing fees** come into play whenever documents need to be officially filed, such as for probate proceedings or guardianships.
- **Document preparation charges** apply even for standard paperwork. Fees can rise if revisions or additions are needed after the initial documents are created.
- **Specialized services** increase the bill. These might include setting up complex trusts, arranging durable power of attorney, or handling advance healthcare directives.
- **Extra or unexpected expenses** show up when documents need amendments, when family disputes arise and spark litigation, or if appraisals must be done for property or family businesses.

Common Cost Traps

Failing to keep legal documents up-to-date is one reason costs spiral. Changes after a marriage, divorce, birth, or significant financial event can require new paperwork, which almost always brings another round of fees. Disagreements between heirs trigger court battles, often making legal costs skyrocket. Unorganized executor appointments result in errors and delays, which invite hours of legal work and additional costs.

Practical Steps to Reduce Legal Expenses

You don't have to accept high bills as a given. Simple actions before and during the estate planning process can save real money.

- **Prepare thoroughly before meeting a professional**
    - Gather all relevant documents: deeds, lists of assets and debts, insurance policies, account statements, and personal identification.
    - Set estate goals: who gets what, who can act for you, and any special requests.
    - Decide who could serve as executor, trustee, or power of attorney based on their organizational and financial skills.
- **Communicate goals from the start**
    - Explain wishes and priorities in the first meeting to avoid unnecessary follow-up sessions.
    - List questions in advance instead of asking them one at a time over several phone calls or emails.
- **Use technology when possible**
    - Reputable online legal platforms allow for simple wills and advance directives at a fraction of the cost of in-person lawyers.
    - For example, a young couple with plain wishes might use an online service to draft wills, but if they own a business or have a blended family, a paid consultation with an attorney remains worthwhile.
- **Ask about fees up front**
    - Get quotes for flat-fee services whenever possible, limiting uncertainty.
    - Compare lawyers or planning firms by their approach to billing—some may offer package deals, while others bill hourly or take a percentage.

- **Leverage community and group resources**
  - Many legal aid clinics, senior centers, or employee assistance programs offer discounted or even free help with estate planning basics.
  - Unions, alumni networks, or professional organizations sometimes provide access to vetted attorneys at special rates.

Illustration: Organized Family, Lower Bill

Imagine a family that reviews and organizes all their account statements, property records, and insurance in advance. They come to the attorney with a clear list of goals and executor choice. This preparation means their lawyer spends less time sorting through paperwork or clarifying intentions, reducing billable hours and keeping the process efficient.

Strategies to Simplify and Avoid Legal Tangles

- Keep beneficiary designations up-to-date on retirement accounts, life insurance policies, and payable-on-death bank accounts. These assets move directly to heirs and often bypass legal wrangling.
- Use joint ownership with rights of survivorship, where appropriate, so property passes directly to the surviving owner.
- Avoid overcomplicating trusts or setting up unnecessary entities unless there are clear benefits. Complexity can lead to confusion, mistakes, and hours of legal fixes.
- Pick executors and powers of attorney for their skills, not just family ties, to cut down on confusion and avoid costly delays.

Planning in this way not only brings peace of mind, but it also shields families from financial shocks at an already stressful time. Looking ahead, the next step involves fitting in financial products such as life insurance to further guard against risks that pure legal planning can't always cover, making sure heirs receive support with less hassle and uncertainty.

Incorporating Life Insurance into Estate Planning

Expenses often follow a person's death, leaving families with sudden legal bills, taxes, or debts that must be settled quickly. Life insurance provides families the cash they need immediately after death, offering an effective way to limit the stress of selling off assets or homes at a loss. When a person passes, life insurance payouts are typically released directly to named beneficiaries. This step bypasses probate, which can drag on for months and generate legal costs. The direct payment of insurance proceeds helps families settle medical bills, funeral costs, mortgages, and estate taxes quickly. Instead of waiting for a court to sort out the estate, families can address these expenses immediately. Having cash available prevents heirs from needing to sell family property, stocks, or treasured items during a tough time.

Life Insurance Benefits for Heirs and Tax Reduction

The death benefit from a life insurance policy also keeps the long-term financial goals of the family in focus. These funds can serve as a bridge for daily expenses, pay for college, or keep up on the mortgage. It's a flexible source of money when heirs might have no other quick access to funds. For example, a family with young children might use the policy's proceeds to fund tuition or childcare. For a couple, the surviving spouse could use insurance to cover monthly bills or retirement savings. This security lessens the chance that surviving family members will face missed opportunities or sudden hardship.

There's also a tax benefit. In most cases, death benefits from life insurance paid to individuals are not counted as taxable income on the federal level. This means heirs receive the full sum without needing to set aside a chunk for the IRS. But estate taxes may apply if the insured owns the policy and the value of the overall estate, including the insurance, crosses a federal estate tax threshold. Some states have their estate or inheritance taxes, which can also affect the payout.

How a policy is owned and who is named as beneficiary makes a difference. To avoid adding insurance proceeds to a taxable estate, many people set up an irrevocable life insurance trust (ILIT). The trust owns the policy; after death, proceeds go to the trust, then to beneficiaries, staying out of the taxable estate.

Example Scenario

Imagine a single parent, Sarah, who owns a $500,000 policy. If she is the owner and the beneficiary is her adult daughter, the payout will be taxed only if Sarah's overall estate is large enough for estate taxes to kick in. Sarah wants to avoid this. She creates an ILIT, which owns the policy. After Sarah's death, her daughter gets the money from the trust without extra estate taxes.

Types of Life Insurance in Estate Planning

Choosing the right life insurance depends on long-term goals and cost. There are two broad types:

- **Term Life Insurance** covers a set period—like twenty years. If death happens during the term, the payout goes to the beneficiaries. These policies are usually less expensive, but once the term ends, coverage and benefits go away. Term insurance often works best for short-term needs or debts with an end date, such as a mortgage.

- **Permanent Life Insurance** (including whole and universal life) doesn't expire if premiums are paid. These policies build cash value over time and guarantee a death benefit no matter when the insured passes away. Permanent insurance costs more but offers certainty for estate planning goals.

For estate planning, permanent policies are favored because they guarantee a payout. For example, John and Lisa want to ensure they leave something for their three children regardless of when they pass. They choose a whole life policy, even though it's pricier. The security outweighs extra premium dollars. On the other hand, Maria, age 44, with two young kids and a tight budget, obtains a twenty-year term policy just to cover her mortgage and childcare while the kids are dependent. For people looking to create a legacy for years to come, permanent insurance better fits the goal.

Integration with the Larger Estate Plan

Life insurance policies work best when woven into the full estate plan. Many people name a trust as the policy's beneficiary. This allows the terms of the trust to control how and when the money gets handed out. For those wanting to support a cause, designating a charity as a beneficiary delivers donations while reducing estate size and possibly lowering taxes. Policy reviews matter, too. Updates may be needed after a birth, death, marriage, or divorce.

Smart use of life insurance brings peace of mind. It offers protection from unexpected taxes, legal bills, or asset sales, supporting every step taken to keep more wealth in the hands of beneficiaries. Careful planning matches the right policy and ownership methods to the needs of each family, reinforcing asset protection and trimming long-term costs.

Bringing It All Together

Now that you understand how estate taxes, legal fees, and life insurance affect your family's financial future, you can take confident steps to protect your assets and reduce unnecessary costs. By planning carefully—using tools like trusts, updating documents regularly, choosing the right beneficiaries, and exploring life insurance options—you can keep more of your estate in your family's hands and avoid costly surprises. This proactive approach not only saves money but also brings peace of mind, ensuring your loved ones are supported without added stress or delays. Taking action today means building a stronger, clearer legacy for tomorrow.

CHAPTER 8
PROTECTING REAL ESTATE AND PROPERTY

The call came late one evening: a family member had passed away unexpectedly, and the house they left behind was suddenly at the center of confusion and conflict. Titles were unclear, documents were scattered, and what should have been a simple transfer of ownership turned into weeks of legal wrangling. Feeling overwhelmed, those left behind soon realized how little they understood about protecting such a valuable asset—and how costly that lack of preparation could become.

This moment is not uncommon. Too often, families lose time, money, and peace because basic steps weren't taken to secure property in advance. But what if there were clear ways to prevent this chaos—tools to organize ownership and strategies to protect assets from unexpected risks? The process may seem complicated, yet with the right guidance and a few deliberate actions, it becomes manageable—providing peace of mind that your property is safeguarded today and ready for tomorrow's uncertainties.

Primary Methods for Safeguarding Property: Trusts, Joint Ownership, and Transfer-on-Death Deeds

Trusts serve as a cornerstone for shielding real estate, providing a way for property owners to avoid probate, increase privacy, and manage their assets both while living and after passing away. Placing a property in a trust involves creating a legal arrangement where someone (the trustee) holds title to the property for the benefit of another person (the beneficiary). One of the most common and practical options is a living revocable trust. In this setup, the property owner usually acts as both trustee and beneficiary during their lifetime, keeping full control of the asset. If incapacity strikes, a successor trustee steps in, allowing for uninterrupted management. When the owner passes away, the successor trustee distributes the property to the named beneficiaries without sending it through probate court.

Setting up a trust starts with choosing the right kind for the owner's goals, most often a revocable living trust for homes intended to pass smoothly to family. The property title changes from the owner's name to the name of the trust, a step that must be reflected in the deed recording. Trust documents must name the trustee and successor trustee and list the beneficiaries. The process centralizes management and control, particularly useful for those with young children, blended families, or anyone who wants to avoid court involvement. Control also extends to possible protection from some creditors who might otherwise target the property. Typically, creating a trust involves some legal paperwork and fees, but the later reduction in court and attorney costs often outweighs these costs.

An example brings this home: a parent sets up a revocable living trust, names their child as the beneficiary, and retitles the family house to the trust. Should the parent pass away or become incapacitated, the successor trustee takes over. When the parent dies, the house passes straight to the child, skipping probate and minimizing both delays and disputes.

Joint ownership takes a different approach, relying on co-ownership arrangements that transfer property automatically at death. There are several ways to structure joint ownership. Joint tenancy with right of survivorship means that when one owner dies, the surviving owner instantly holds full title. Tenancy by the entirety applies to married couples in some states, providing similar survivorship rights along with added protection from creditors. Tenancy in common, while allowing shared ownership, does not ensure automatic transfer or survivorship; each owner can instead pass their fractional share to beneficiaries in their will.

The primary advantage of joint tenancy and tenancy by the entirety lies in their straightforward nature. Once established by titling the deed correctly, no extra paperwork or legal action is needed after one co-owner dies. Ownership simply continues with the survivor, trimming away court fees and delays. These structures are affordable to set up, because transferring to joint ownership is often just a matter of recording a new deed. Yet practical risks exist. If one co-owner faces lawsuits, divorces, or debts, the property could be at risk from their creditors. Disagreements or changes in family relationships may also create tension or legal fights down the line.

This is seen when two siblings inherit their childhood home as joint tenants. Years later, one passes away. The survivor instantly controls the property, and the house never enters probate, avoiding a tangle of paperwork and family disputes.

Adding to the toolkit, transfer-on-death (TOD) deeds offer a "payable on death" style solution for real estate, now recognized in many states. A TOD deed lets an owner name a beneficiary who will receive the property the moment the owner dies, avoiding probate. Setting one up means filling out a form deed with the correct beneficiary name and recording it at the local land records office. The owner can amend or revoke the deed anytime before death, preserving complete authority during their life.

TOD deeds offer several clear upsides. Property owners keep autonomy, pay few costs, and sidestep the probate system. But pitfalls arise if the owner moves or changes beneficiaries and fails to update the deed. Only a limited number of states allow TOD deeds for real property. For example, a parent records a TOD deed directing their house to a son. Upon the parent's death, the property is transferred directly and immediately to the child without legal battles or any court filings.

Choosing a method starts with personal goals and family needs:

- For those wanting control, privacy, and flexibility for complex families, trusts are the best fit.
- If easy, inexpensive transfer to a spouse or single heir is the goal and all parties get along, joint ownership can work.
- For those who want simple, low-cost solutions and live in a TOD-eligible state, the TOD deed streamlines everything.

Here's a checklist for getting started:

- Decide on the right method for your property and family plan
- Gather key documents and check your state's laws
- Complete all forms, deed transfers, or trust paperwork fully and accurately
- Record documents with your county or city land office
- Review your arrangements every few years or after major life changes

Laying this foundation for the family home means basic risks are handled, making it easier to focus on other properties where extra exposure, debts, or rental rules often matter. Vacation homes and rentals sometimes call for layered or staggered protection using different versions of these strategies.

Protecting Second Homes and Rental Properties: Unique Considerations and Strategies

Protecting a non-primary residence demands a shift in strategy from the approaches used for your main home. While methods such as using a trust, setting up joint ownership, or naming a transfer-on-death beneficiary work well for shielding your primary residence, second homes or investment properties introduce fresh opportunities and new kinds of risks. These homes may sit vacant for stretches, host renters, or operate across state lines, each scenario bringing its set of exposures. Because of this, the protection plan needs to expand and adapt.

Owning a rental property or vacation home can create steady income or serve as a family getaway. Yet, alongside the rewards, these properties introduce new growth, disruption, and uncertainty. Three main risk areas deserve attention: tenant issues, liability from incidents on the property, and challenges driven by the property's region or local law.

Tenant Risks

Tenant issues can cause headaches. Renters sometimes damage property, miss payments, or start legal disputes. To lower these risks, focus first on clear paperwork. A detailed lease agreement spells out the renter's responsibilities, covers security deposit requirements, sets rules about subletting, and describes exactly what counts as property damage. Strong, clear language reduces confusion and gives you a tool to back up claims if something goes wrong.

It helps to include check-in and check-out inspection forms within the lease. These forms record the condition of the rooms, appliances, and fixtures, leaving less room for disagreement. If a renter tries to dispute charges or blame you for damage, the signed documents provide support.

Liability Exposure

Liability risks go beyond everyday wear and tear. Guests, workers, or neighbors could suffer injury while on your property, leading to lawsuits or insurance claims. Holding your real estate through a business entity, like a limited liability company (LLC), can create a shield. With an LLC, legal action against the property stops at the business and typically cannot reach your personal assets.

Setting up an LLC requires registration with your state and regular updates—but the paperwork pays off. For example, an owner who held his duplex in an LLC faced a tenant lawsuit after a slip on icy stairs. Because the LLC owned the duplex, the suit targeted the company and not his family's personal savings or primary home.

Insuring the property properly finishes the shield. Regular homeowners insurance does not always cover rental situations or cover income lost when a vacation property shuts down after storm damage. Landlord insurance fills in those gaps and covers risks from tenants. An umbrella policy stretches liability protection further, often adding millions in extra coverage for a modest cost. If you let friends use your property or rent it out on short-term platforms, ask your insurer about adding riders for those purposes.

A property-specific rider can handle issues unique to your area. After a hurricane, for instance, a vacation homeowner with a storm coverage rider received quick payment for roof repairs, avoiding months of lost income.

Regional Concerns

Local laws can affect your rental or second home. Zoning, noise rules, and restrictions by homeowner associations can lead to fines or forced changes. Short-term rental bans are spreading, while some areas demand extra permits or limit how long tenants can stay.

Stay organized by keeping a copy of all local rules relevant to your address. Reach out to the city or HOA before making changes or renting to check for new requirements.

Titling Ownership and Structure

The way you hold title matters. For a vacation home used only by family, sole or joint ownership may work fine. If you want relatives to inherit it easily, adding the house to a living trust keeps it out of probate court. For rentals, an LLC usually offers more protection. Compare fees, local laws, and how easily you can access equity when picking your structure.

Keep everything current. If you change the use of the property—for instance, switching from family use to regular rental—update the ownership structure, lease forms, and insurance to match.

Action Checklist

- Draft a thorough lease agreement with inspection forms
- Hold rental properties in an LLC for liability protection
- Maintain landlord insurance, property rider, and umbrella policy
- Choose a titling method that matches the specific use and ownership goals
- Gather and update copies of all zoning, permit, and HOA rules
- Review and refresh documents whenever the property's use changes

Careful organization and ongoing updates help each property stay protected under changing circumstances. Keeping all records, coverage, and ownership forms clear will make the next phase—recordkeeping and documentation—much easier and more effective.

Maintaining Security with Proper Documentation: The Importance of Updated and Recorded Paperwork

Keeping property investments safe depends on more than sturdy locks and good insurance. Staying diligent with documentation forms the backbone of property protection, no matter if you own your family home, a vacation house, or a rental property. Properties such as second homes or rentals often come with distinct risks: ownership changes, multiple users, or extended periods where the owner is not present heighten the potential for mistakes or fraud if paperwork falls out of order. A strong habit of reviewing and organizing property records builds a secure foundation that lasts through major life events and changes in ownership.

Property paperwork includes several must-review documents. Deeds and titles prove who owns the property and show its legal description. Mortgage statements reveal any outstanding loans or liens and highlight the financial obligations attached to the property. Insurance policies detail what is covered in the event of damage or disaster. Trust declarations, beneficiary designations, and any amendments document the current legal status and any instructions for future transfer. Also, keep records of property taxes paid, utility bills that establish occupancy, and any documents from county recorders or local governments about your property. Every name, address, date, and legal description should be consistent across all these files. Even a small error, such as a misspelled name or an old address, can lead to confusion or legal hurdles in the future.

Unchecked or outdated paperwork can introduce costly setbacks. For example, if a property deed lists the wrong owner or address, family members may face probate delays or fail to inherit assets as intended. An old mortgage statement that is not replaced after refinancing might misrepresent current debts, slowing down the sale or transfer of a home. An unrecorded transfer to a trust can leave an estate open to legal battle, even if the owner's wishes were clear. Cases like these end up in court, taking months or years to resolve, and often bring high legal costs or lasting friction between heirs. Equally, unmonitored records increase vulnerability to identity theft or fraudulent transfer attempts that can put property ownership at risk.

Making organization a routine stops these problems before they start. Start by creating a master file for each property you own, both in physical form—using a locked file cabinet or safe deposit box—and digitally, with backup copies stored in encrypted cloud accounts or on reliable drives. Group records by type: deeds and titles in one folder, mortgage and lien statements in another, insurance paperwork in a third, and all supporting documents—like tax records and correspondence with officials—in labeled subfolders. Color-coding or using digital tags can help you spot missing paperwork quickly.

Set calendar reminders once or twice a year to review your property files. During each review, confirm that all names appear exactly as they should, dates are current, descriptions match the latest legal survey or appraisal, and supporting bills or receipts have no gaps. If you spot any outdated paperwork, contact the source—whether that's your mortgage company, insurance agent, or county recorder—for an updated version and replace the old documents in your files. Keep a log with each record, noting when it was last reviewed or updated, along with the name and contact information of the official or agent you spoke with.

Original documents, such as signed deeds or trust declarations, deserve special care. Store them somewhere both secure and accessible, such as a fireproof safe at home or a safe deposit box at your bank. Make copies for everyday reference and provide a trusted person, such as your attorney or adult child, instructions on where to find the originals in an emergency.

Some events force updates. If you get married, divorced, or widowed, update deeds, titles, and insurance beneficiaries promptly. After refinancing a mortgage, add the new statement and remove the old one. If you transfer your property into a trust or change a beneficiary, double-check that every record reflects this. When an owner dies, submit required forms to official agencies and request updated documentation showing the rightful new owner or trustee. Waiting can cause complications that delay sales, inheritance, or insurance payouts.

A few warning signs call for immediate review. These include mismatched names or addresses between documents, notifications about liens you did not authorize, errors on statements, or legal papers arriving about your property. Any change in your personal information, like a new last name, also requires careful checking to avoid errors that can spiral into larger issues.

Making these routines a habit is easier with practical systems. Try using cloud storage services with bank-level security for digital copies, investing in a safe deposit box for originals, and reviewing property management or document tracking apps. Develop a checklist of required records so you know at a glance what needs updating. Taking these steps makes property ownership more secure and helps protect your investment—and your loved ones' peace of mind—long into the future.

Final Thoughts

Now that you understand the key strategies and practical steps for protecting your real estate and property assets, you are better equipped to create a secure plan tailored to your family's needs and goals. Whether choosing trusts for control and privacy, joint ownership for simplicity, or transfer-on-death deeds for straightforward transfers, taking action will help you avoid costly legal delays and protect your investment against unexpected challenges. Maintaining accurate, up-to-date documentation and regularly reviewing your arrangements ensures your plan stays strong through life's changes. By applying these tools thoughtfully, you can safeguard your property, reduce stress for your loved ones, and build a lasting legacy with confidence and peace of mind.

CHAPTER 9
DIGITAL ESTATE PLANNING – WHAT HAPPENS TO YOUR ONLINE LIFE?

"Did you ever think about what happens to your email, social media, or online bank accounts if something happens to you? Most of us have dozens of digital accounts that hold more than just passwords—they contain memories, money, and personal information. Yet, many people haven't made plans for who will manage these assets or how they will be protected in the future. As technology becomes a bigger part of our daily lives, understanding how to organize and secure your online presence is no longer optional—it's essential. This chapter guides you through the steps to take control of your digital legacy, so your loved ones won't face confusion or loss when they need access most."

Managing Digital Assets and Setting Up Legacy Access

A **digital asset** is any online record, account, file, or collection connected to your name or finances. These range from online bank accounts and brokerage logins, which hold direct financial value, to cloud services like Google Drive or Dropbox, where family photos or important documents may be stored. Email accounts, utility bill portals, loyalty rewards memberships, streaming subscriptions, and social media profiles are all part of your digital footprint. Some assets, like PayPal or Venmo accounts, contain funds or transaction histories that affect ongoing business or estate matters. Others, such as Facebook pages or digital music libraries, hold personal meaning or purchased content you wouldn't want to lose. It's also easy to overlook domain names, personal websites, and cryptocurrency wallets, yet losing access to them can mean permanent loss of money or irreplaceable memories.

The value of these assets goes far beyond dollars. Personal emails may include family correspondence or legal notifications. Digital photo libraries can represent decades of memories—imagine the heartbreak if no one could retrieve them after a death. Cryptocurrency wallets, protected only by private keys, are often lost forever without proper documentation. It's common for relatives to find themselves unable to unlock a parent's photo backup or locate an account number for a digital brokerage. Even loyalty points, hotel rewards, or frequent flyer miles may be transferable, adding to potential losses when records aren't tracked.

With so many accounts to manage, **password organization** becomes one of the biggest challenges. Many people reuse a few passwords or jot them down on paper, but these methods fail when someone else needs access in an emergency. Frequent resets and varying requirements add confusion. The average person now manages dozens of logins, each demanding strong, unique credentials to reduce the risk of fraud or hacking. Yet while complex passwords keep intruders out, they can also lock out your family.

Password managers help solve this problem. Services like LastPass, 1Password, and Bitwarden create a secure digital vault where every login, password, and note is encrypted and protected by one strong master password that only you know. Inside, you can store credentials for all accounts, generate new passwords, and organize entries by category or use. Many managers allow sharing access with trusted contacts through built-in tools. For estate planning, this vault becomes a kind of master key—if a designated executor knows how to access it, your entire online world remains reachable when needed.

Setting up a password manager usually involves these steps:

1. Choose a reputable password manager and create your account.
2. Choose a long, unique master password you won't forget.
3. Import or manually add credentials for each digital account.
4. Group accounts by category or add notes for context.
5. Enable any "emergency access," "family sharing," or backup features.

It's essential to protect and document your master password or any emergency recovery methods. Keep printed instructions sealed in a safe or lockbox, and consider having a second copy in another secure location. Naming a reliable contact who can assist—preferably someone who understands privacy—helps keep everything accessible in case of urgent need.

Large companies now recognize the importance of digital inheritance. Many major platforms include settings to designate successors or give limited access after an account becomes inactive. For example, Google's Inactive Account Manager lets you choose trusted people to get notified or receive selected data if your account is unused for a period. Facebook allows you to select a Legacy Contact, empowering them to manage your memorialized profile or download shared material. Apple offers a Digital Legacy feature, enabling a nominated person to retrieve your iCloud data after a review period. It's wise to regularly review and update these settings to match changing relationships or asset values. Naming more than one trusted contact lowers the chance that no one can act if the main contact is unavailable.

A solid organizational system supports all of these solutions. Start by listing all digital assets in a spreadsheet, a secure note, or an encrypted file. Categories might be:

- Financial: banks, investments, crypto wallets
- Communication: email, social platforms, chat accounts
- Media: photos, music, book collections
- Utilities and Services: bills, reward programs

Include short notes for each—why it matters, its approximate value, and tips for accessing it. If using hard copies, keep them in a locked drawer or safe deposit box, not in a public spot. Only share these lists, or vault passwords, with individuals who really need access, sticking to the principle of least privilege to limit privacy risk.

Planning these steps protects your legacy and privacy. Loved ones aren't left lost, guessing at passwords or unable to claim what you built. With accounts mapped and tools in place, you're ready to document wishes for each digital asset and designate heirs or managers according to your values. This clarity makes the next phase of planning direct and manageable.

Creating a Comprehensive Digital Estate Plan

Building on your work cataloging digital assets, it's now time to turn that careful inventory into a detailed plan that secures your digital life for yourself and those you care about. Knowing exactly which bank accounts, cloud storage logins, social media profiles, and other online services you use gives you a strong foundation to decide what should happen to each one. Some accounts, like family email addresses or shared photo libraries, might hold sentimental value and need special handling. Others, such as investment platforms, business websites, or cryptocurrency wallets, could have financial consequences if left unmanaged or inaccessible. In chapter 10, we will discuss the legal landscape surrounding digital estates, privacy regulations, and the impact of platform terms of service on access to online accounts after death.

Start by documenting every asset on your list in a way that's clear and easy for someone else to understand. Use practical details for each: for a bank login, note not just the website address and username, but also how you currently access it (for example, via an authenticator app, saved phone number, or separate two-factor device). For photo libraries, list the cloud provider, the account email, and note if you've enabled automatic backups. Is it a personal account, for family, or business? Is it active, or has it gone unused for years? Write down which ones you check weekly, which sit dormant, and any you only use for work or gig jobs. If you aren't sure whether you still have access to an old account, or can't remember its password, set aside time to recover or delete it—this step will save your loved ones confusion later. If you run across accounts you forgot about, add them to your list and close any you no longer need.

For each item, include backup steps where needed, such as printing recovery codes for a password manager, storing seed words for a crypto wallet offline, or noting where two-factor authentication settings are kept. If your phone is essential for authentication, decide if it's labeled clearly somewhere. Keeping these details organized now keeps everything smoother for whoever steps in later, whether that's next month during a move, or years down the line when someone else needs to pick up the pieces.

As you review your inventory, think about who is best suited to inherit or shut down each kind of asset. The right digital steward often depends on the account type and what you want done with it. A sibling who works in IT might be perfect for handling encrypted files, while a friend who understands social media could help with memorial pages or removing private content. For investment apps or payment accounts, pick someone financially savvy who can follow proper closure steps and notify other stakeholders if needed. You might want different people for different jobs; that's fine. The main goal is that each digital asset has a clear, named person responsible and a written action: archive, delete, transfer, or just monitor.

Instructions should be specific: avoid saying "deal with my emails" and instead write, for example, "forward any emails from my accountant to my spouse, then close the account," or "preserve my wedding photos in Google Photos and share access with my children." A written list of wishes—rather than general requests—reduces the risk of loved ones guessing what you wanted or arguing about how something should be handled. Suppose you ran a personal blog for years, kept active social media accounts, and invested in stocks through a phone app. You may wish for your blog to be archived, your Facebook set to memorial, and your brokerage apps to be closed securely after the balance is settled. Each of these choices needs a contact name, access method, and clear instruction.

After deciding on heirs and actions, organize your directives as simply as possible. You can use a typed sheet, a handwritten page, an easy spreadsheet, or even a secure digital note, as long as the information is orderly: asset name, access steps, responsible contact, and intended action. Update these regularly; a good habit is to pick a recurring date—such as a birthday, tax time, or start of a new year—to review your documents and make changes. Store one digital copy in a secure cloud folder and print a version for your estate binder or safe deposit box so they're accessible even if your devices change.

Exercise — Build Your Digital Estate Plan

Prepare your own digital estate plan one step at a time. Break it into 20-minute sessions if it feels overwhelming.

1. Gather your asset list with account names and uses.
2. For each asset, add access details (login paths, devices used, backup codes if any).
3. Match each asset to a trusted contact and write a simple action (archive, delete, transfer).

4. Organize your notes: a spreadsheet, worksheet, or notebook.
5. Share the document's location with your designated digital heirs.
6. Set a calendar reminder to review this plan every 6–12 months.

Sample Entry:

- Asset: Gmail (Personal)
- Access: gmail.com, username, password manager, backup code in safe
- Contact: Angela (daughter)
- Action: Forward important messages to spouse, then close account

Follow these steps to give both yourself and your loved ones peace of mind about your digital life, knowing your wishes are clear, organized, and up to date.

Understanding Legal Considerations and Privacy Implications

When people finish recording their wishes and digital account details, they face a new challenge: navigating the maze of laws, privacy rules, and company policies that govern digital estate planning. It isn't enough to tell someone what you want done with your online accounts—legal restrictions and platform policies determine what an executor or loved one can actually do with digital assets.

Privacy and data protection laws set real limits. In the United States, the **Stored Communications Act (SCA)** restricts a service provider's ability to share email contents or private messages, even when there's a court order or written will. Companies like Google and Apple rely on this law to block unauthorized access, meaning heirs may be denied entry to cloud-based emails or drive files. In the

European Union, the **General Data Protection Regulation (GDPR)** imposes strict rules on personal data, often making it difficult for families to access accounts unless the original owner planned ahead. Many U.S. states have their own laws as well. For example, the **Revised Uniform Fiduciary Access to Digital Assets Act (RUFADAA)** grants executors or agents limited legal authority to manage digital assets—but only if explicit permission is given in legal documents.

Having a will or power of attorney doesn't guarantee access to everything online. When digital lives are tied to major platforms, their **terms of service** become the real gatekeepers. These contracts often state that accounts are licensed, not owned, allowing companies to restrict, suspend, or delete them at their discretion. For instance, Apple requires a court order and specific legal filings before releasing data from a deceased user's account, regardless of family wishes. Facebook lets users appoint a **Legacy Contact** to manage a memorialized profile but blocks access to private messages. Google's **Inactive Account Manager** allows a designated person to receive certain data after a set period of inactivity, but only for information the user marked as shareable. Executors who overlook these built-in tools may find themselves locked out, even with perfectly prepared legal documents.

Real-world cases reveal how powerful these digital barriers can be. Families have permanently lost years of shared photos when cloud storage companies refused access and no backup existed. In other cases, executors holding court orders, wills, and even passwords were still denied entry to a deceased person's email because company policy outweighed legal authority. When cryptocurrency wallets are involved, a missing password or seed phrase can erase entire fortunes—these assets often exist beyond the reach of both courts and estate law.

To reduce these risks and protect privacy, integrate safeguards directly into your digital estate plan. **Appoint a digital executor** and name that person in your legal documents to signal authorization to both courts and companies. This executor should know which accounts include legacy or inactive-manager tools and be ready to use them. When setting up features such as Google's Inactive Account Manager or Facebook's Legacy Contact, follow the platform's instructions precisely. Use two-factor authentication only where it won't interfere with access, and document where authentication keys or backup codes are stored. Never include passwords directly in wills or legal papers. Instead, store them securely in a **password manager**, and provide access instructions separately, in accordance with each service's policies.

Privacy does not end with death or incapacity. Someone's digital past—emails, messages, posts, and photos—can become public, misused, or lost if not handled with care. Imagine a scenario where an executor shares access too widely, and private family matters reach the wrong people. Or, where a law changes, and something once locked becomes open to others. Periodically review all plans, making sure account settings, privacy controls, and legal documents match current laws and platform rules. Most companies adjust service terms, privacy protections, and inheritance features over time. Ongoing checks are the only way to close gaps and stop surprises.

Laws and company rules will not always match personal wishes. Some assets—like certain online subscriptions or digital content—may not transfer at all under current laws. The safest path is making sure trusted people have legal authority, are trained in platform tools, and keep up with updates. Discussing these choices with loved ones and updating plans when laws or terms change provides peace of mind that your digital estate will be protected and respected the way you want.

Final Thoughts

Now that you understand the importance of managing and organizing your digital assets, you can take confident steps to protect your online presence for the future. By carefully documenting your accounts, setting up secure password management, and naming trusted contacts, you create a clear roadmap that guides your loved ones in carrying out your wishes with minimal stress and confusion. Staying informed about legal and privacy issues ensures your plan remains effective amid changing laws and platform rules. With an up-to-date digital estate plan in place, you safeguard not only financial assets but also cherished memories, providing peace of mind that your digital legacy will be respected and preserved.

CHAPTER 10
FAMILY CONVERSATIONS AND AVOIDING CONFLICT

"Why are we even talking about this now?" my sister asked, her voice tight with frustration. The room felt heavy as the words hung between us, an uncomfortable silence settling in afterward. I understood her hesitation—estate planning isn't easy to bring up, especially when emotions run high and relationships feel fragile. Yet avoiding the conversation doesn't erase the questions or concerns; it only leaves them simmering beneath the surface, ready to ignite at the worst possible time. These family talks are not just about dividing assets—they touch on trust, fairness, and the future of those we care about most. Facing them head-on takes courage, patience, and a clear approach that invites everyone in rather than shutting them out.

Communicating Your Plans and Involving Heirs Early

Some families delay estate planning discussions because they fear it will spark arguments, reopen old wounds, or stir uncomfortable emotions. Many adults worry that bringing it up will lead to hurt feelings or make it seem like they're planning for someone's absence too soon. Yet avoiding these talks often leads to silent misunderstandings, confusion, and conflict later—precisely when clarity is needed most. Open, honest conversations about estate plans give everyone a chance to understand, adjust, and contribute, preventing frustration and suspicion before they take root. Families who discuss these matters early and often often end up feeling more united and prepared, confident there won't be unpleasant surprises down the road.

Discussing estate planning is rarely easy, even among close families. Parents may dread their children questioning decisions about who inherits the house, the family business, or treasured keepsakes. Adult children, in turn, might fear appearing greedy or upsetting their parents by raising the topic at all. Beneath these worries usually lies a sincere desire to avoid pain, protect relationships, and ensure fairness for everyone involved.

What helps most is a clear, proactive approach that removes guesswork and invites participation. When everyone knows where they stand, they can plan together with confidence instead of speculating in silence. Including heirs and other key people early in the process makes a major difference. Once family members feel that decisions are being made behind closed doors, trust begins to erode—making any outcome feel unfair, even when it isn't. Early inclusion fosters shared purpose and reassurance instead of fear or resentment.

Consider a family who chooses to share their estate plans during a holiday gathering. Instead of waiting until someone asks or until a crisis forces the issue, the parents prepare a brief summary explaining how they want to divide property, what guided their choices, and which keepsakes hold special meaning. Each child has the opportunity to ask questions, share thoughts, or express interest in particular items. Everyone leaves the table feeling relieved, included, and more at peace about the future.

Practical Communication Tools for Estate Planning

Open communication takes intention and clear steps. Here are several practical strategies that help guide these sensitive discussions:

- **Schedule a dedicated family meeting** for estate planning, rather than mentioning it in passing. This signals respect for everyone's time and attention and sets aside a safe space for discussion.
- **Prepare a clear agenda** listing topics such as the will, trusts, healthcare decisions, and treasured possessions. Inform family members about the topic of discussion to avoid surprising them.
- **Explain your reasoning** for major decisions. For example, "We want the house to go to you because you have been living here and caring for it," or "We chose this executor because they understand financial matters."
- **Use plain language.** Avoid legal and financial jargon whenever possible, so no one feels left out or misunderstood.
- **Listen actively.** Give people time to share questions or worries without jumping in with answers or dismissing concerns.
- **Validate emotions.** If someone seems anxious or upset, acknowledge their feelings. Say, for instance, "I can see this makes you uncomfortable. Can you tell me what's concerning you?"
- **Invite honest feedback.** Encourage everyone to speak up if something doesn't feel right. This gives a chance to resolve tension early, rather than during a crisis later.

When a difficult topic arises—such as differing opinions about a family property or a child's worry about being left out—direct acknowledgment works best. If a child expresses fear that an inheritance will be unfair, the parent might say, "I understand why you're worried. Let's talk about how we came to this decision and see if we can address your concerns together." Including everyone's views shows respect and increases the sense of fairness.

Keeping the Conversation Going

One meeting is not always enough. Families grow, life circumstances change, and plans may need to be updated. Build trust further by establishing regular check-ins—perhaps once a year or after major events—to review plans, answer new questions, and share any adjustments. Keep written notes or a simple summary of each meeting, then distribute them to everyone. Documenting what was discussed and agreed on gives people peace of mind and reduces confusion.

Picture a family that gathers once every spring to revisit their estate plan. The parents share updates, invite questions, and give each child a copy of any changes. If a grandchild is born or someone's financial situation shifts, the family discusses how to reflect that in new arrangements.

Sometimes, openness does not prevent every disagreement. Some topics stay emotional, and resistance may surface anyway. Readers will need practical tools for addressing difficult reactions, which shapes the path forward for working through conflict and building lasting family trust.

Managing Resistance, Emotions, and Disagreements

Open and honest dialogue is more than a courtesy during estate planning—it builds the trust needed to navigate emotional reactions. When everyone feels heard and understood, even difficult conversations become easier to manage. Openness lays the groundwork for empathy, helping families face emotionally charged moments with clarity instead of frustration. For many adults, talking about inheritance, wills, or future care can stir strong feelings or surface old misunderstandings. These topics often touch deep insecurities, leading people to react defensively or withdraw. By focusing on clear and gentle communication, you create an atmosphere where emotional resistance has less power.

Estate planning conversations can trigger emotion for many reasons. Sibling rivalries may resurface when discussing how assets will be divided. One sibling might recall feeling overlooked or less favored, becoming more sensitive to perceived unfairness. Distrust can stem from old patterns—childhood conflicts over money or disagreements about how property was handled after a previous loss. Fear of being excluded is common, especially if adult children worry about their place in the family's future. Grief also plays a role, as reminders of aging or past losses can bring sadness close to the surface. Old resentments—about caregiving, support, or earlier disputes—can unexpectedly influence today's discussions. When families begin dividing property, memories of what mattered most often rise up, touching each person's sense of identity, belonging, or fairness.

Anger in these moments might sound like sharp words or heated arguments about what is "fair." Denial can appear as avoidance—refusing to engage, changing the subject, or insisting it's "too soon" to talk. Anxiety may show up through fidgeting, repeated questions, or indecision. Some people become defensive, interpreting questions as personal criticism. Others withdraw completely—falling silent or leaving the room to avoid pain. Imagine an adult son raising his voice as his parents explain their plans; he might feel his role in the family slipping away or believe his efforts are being overlooked. A daughter may grow quiet when her siblings discuss selling the family home if she associates that house with her childhood security.

There are reliable ways to navigate these challenging moments. The first is **active listening**—listening carefully, pausing before replying, and restating what you've heard to show understanding. For example: *"It sounds like you're worried about being left out of decisions. Is that right?"* This approach demonstrates that you value their feelings, even if you don't agree. When people feel understood, they often relax, opening the door to real conversation.

Staying calm under pressure is another skill worth developing. Practicing deliberate breathing—slow, steady breaths—can stop tension from escalating. Calling a brief time-out can also help; stepping away for a few minutes allows everyone to regain composure. For instance, if the discussion turns heated, you might say, *"Let's take a short break. I want to keep this conversation respectful."*

Framing difficult topics carefully reduces defensiveness. Begin with a clear purpose rather than blame or accusation. For example: *"My goal is to make sure everyone understands Dad's wishes so no one feels confused later."* Or, *"I want us all to feel this is as fair as possible."* Framing the conversation around shared understanding makes it easier for everyone to stay focused on solutions instead of feeling judged.

Defusing tension often means steering the conversation back to shared values or family goals. If an argument over asset division starts to boil, reminding everyone, "We all want to honor Mom's values and keep our family ties strong," can redirect focus. Grounding discussion in common reasons—the desire for fairness, clarity, and ongoing connection—eases the sense of competition or threat.

Recognizing emotional triggers helps families avoid missteps. Sometimes, simple misunderstandings become big problems. If one sibling feels accused when the discussion is only about process, clarifying intentions matters. For instance: "I'm not questioning your responsibility—I only want to make sure each person has input." Stating intentions openly can stop defensive reactions before they start.

Sometimes, strong feelings or repeated dead-ends signal the need for professional help. This can show up as the same fight erupting at every meeting or a family member raising past hurts that cannot be resolved in conversation. When this happens, mediators, family therapists, or neutral estate planning advisors can guide the group.

These professionals offer skills in managing conflict and keeping family discussions on track.

These tools empower you to manage family conversations with respect and effectiveness. By applying these techniques, you build not only agreement in the moment but also a strong foundation for future cooperation. When everyone understands the facts, intentions, and documents involved, future misunderstandings and conflicts become much easier to prevent—shaping a smoother path for estate planning and family harmony.

Creating Clarity to Prevent Future Conflicts

When families talk about estate planning, misunderstandings can cause lasting harm. Emotional topics sometimes lead to confusion or frustration, but a plan that spells out everything in plain words makes a real difference. Families find peace when no one has to guess what a loved one meant. That kind of certainty comes from clear, written instructions that leave nothing unsaid.

Some families discover this lesson through difficult experiences. Imagine siblings arguing after a parent's death because the will said, "split belongings equally," but did not list sentimental items. One child wants the family piano, another thinks it should go to whoever took care of it most, and everyone resents each other. Another family faces trouble when a parent's will names two people as guardians "if possible," with no other details. The uncertainty leads to arguments, legal bills, and hurt feelings that could last for years. Both families could have avoided these problems by spelling out their wishes in plain, detailed language and keeping clear, up-to-date records.

Clear estate planning starts with simple, direct words for every gift and request. Instead of saying, "Leave my jewelry to my children," list each piece and who should get it. Even small keepsakes cause big arguments when wishes are vague. If one child receives a treasured ring, explain in writing why you made this choice—maybe it was promised years ago, or it holds special meaning. Address things people may question. For example, if one child receives a larger share or a special gift, offer a note explaining your reasoning. Simple acts like this reduce hard feelings and give you a chance to share your values.

Ambiguity can also creep into the way people word gifts or divide assets. Avoid broad language like "as they see fit" or "to be shared fairly." Instead, specify either "my wedding album for my oldest daughter, Sarah Smith" or "the contents of my garage for my son, James Smith." Think about scenarios where things could go wrong. If you own a business, say exactly how you want it managed, sold, or handed down. Mention minority owners, outside partners, or key employees by name and say what will happen to their shares. Address the fate of second homes, vacation properties, or family land, including who will pay for upkeep and how you want the use decided.

There are steps that make sure your wishes remain clear and enforced. Keep all papers in an easy-to-find spot, like a fireproof box at home, or at your attorney's office. Here's how to manage your documents effectively:

Keep These Estate Planning Essentials

- Will (with clear, updated instructions)
- Trust documents (if set up)
- Letters of instruction for specific decisions
- List of assets and debts
- Copies of beneficiary forms for insurance and retirement accounts
- List of guardians, executors, trustees, and their contact details
- Power of attorney and medical directive paperwork
- List of professional contacts (attorney, accountant, insurance agent)times

After any big change—birth, marriage, divorce, or loss—look at your paperwork. Cross out the outdated details and write new instructions. If you moved, sold property, or made a major gift, make sure your plan matches your current situation.

Some areas almost always cause stress without guidelines. Blended families need extra care. If you want stepchildren to inherit, name them just as you do biological children. Avoid phrases like "all my children" unless you list everyone clearly. When it comes to family businesses, say who manages them, buys out shares, or receives profits—and what happens if there are disputes. For real estate, write what happens if someone wants to sell, but others do not. This prevents fights and court cases later.

- Some an unequal split is best for your family, but this can sting unless you explain your choice. Leave a letter behind that addresses your decisions in your own words. For example: "I am leaving my house to Sam because he cared for me and maintained the property. My other children receive extra cash to balance the gift."

People want to do the right thing, but they need guidance. Hold a family meeting before anything is final. Share your plan, tell your heirs where your records live, and let them ask questions. To keep the conversation positive, focus on why you made your choices, offer to answer concerns, and make it clear you want to avoid confusion. Sometimes these meetings feel tough, but they pay off by stopping arguments before they start.

Every important conversation, choice, or change should be written down and attached to your other papers. This means leaving a dated note whenever you update your wishes or talk about the estate plan with your family. These written records give your executors and heirs clear, strong proof of your intentions, so your voice remains steady and unmistakable even when you are gone.

Final Thoughts

Now that we understand the importance of open communication, managing emotions, and creating clear, detailed plans, we can approach estate planning with confidence and care. By involving family members early and speaking honestly, we build trust and reduce the chances of future disputes. Using practical tools to listen actively, address concerns gently, and document decisions clearly helps protect relationships and ensures everyone knows what to expect. With these strategies in place, you can create an estate plan that not only safeguards your assets but also strengthens your family's unity and peace of mind for years to come.

CHAPTER 11

KEEPING EVERYTHING ORGANIZED AND ACCESSIBLE

When a family suddenly faces the loss of a loved one, the last thing they need is confusion over important papers. Yet, all too often, critical documents like wills or powers of attorney are missing or hidden in unexpected places. One family spent weeks searching through offices and safety deposit boxes before finding a needed will tucked away in a forgotten briefcase. This delay added cost and deepened the stress during an already difficult time. Many people do not realize how easily such situations arise simply because estate plans are not kept in clear, accessible order. Without a reliable system for storing and sharing these documents, families can struggle to follow instructions or gain access when it matters most. These challenges highlight just how vital careful organization is to ensuring that your wishes are respected and that your loved ones are supported when you can no longer guide them yourself.

Storing Your Documents and Creating an Estate Binder

When life changes suddenly, families often find themselves searching for vital papers at the worst possible moments. One adult daughter recalled how, after her father's passing, no one could locate his original will. It took weeks of anxious searching and repeated trips to local banks before a copy finally turned up in an overlooked briefcase—causing costly legal delays and frayed nerves. This kind of confusion is entirely preventable. When records are organized, your instructions are easy to find and follow. Loved ones gain clarity, avoid guesswork, and spare themselves stress and unnecessary expense. Good organization becomes a quiet act of care—one that keeps chaos at bay when it matters most.

Strong organization begins with gathering every piece of your estate plan. Start by collecting the legal documents: your will, any trust agreements, power of attorney forms, and advance healthcare directives. Then add supporting materials such as insurance policies, property titles and deeds, beneficiary designation forms, bank and investment account details, and lists of passwords and key contacts. When everything sits together in one place, updates become simpler—and more importantly, those who must act on your behalf will have the information they need right away.

Begin assembling your **estate binder** by choosing a sturdy, spacious binder or legacy folder—something durable enough to protect the contents and easy to handle. Add wide dividers or color-coded tabs to separate each section for quick reference. Consider the following divisions:

- Legal Documents (will, trusts, powers of attorney)
- Financial Accounts (bank statements, investment notes)
- Beneficiary Forms and Insurance Policies
- Medical Information (advance directives, Do Not Resuscitate orders)
- Property Records (house deeds, car titles)
- Key Contacts (lawyer, accountant, financial advisor, family names and numbers)
- Personal Instructions (letters to family, digital account information, passwords)

Slip a simple checklist or table of contents at the front. This page offers a snapshot of what's inside and eases the process of checking for missing paperwork when you update things down the road.

Choose a home for your binder that balances safety with accessibility. A locked filing cabinet, fireproof safe, or secure drawer works well. Avoid bank safe deposit boxes—families often struggle to access them at critical moments if the account holder isn't present. Pick a location that's protected from water or fire, yet easy enough for trusted people to find when needed.

Physical folders are only half the story. Back up your estate plan with **digital copies** to protect against loss or damage. Begin by scanning signed, finalized versions of every important document. Many home printers have built-in scanners, or you can use free phone apps for this task. Save the files on an external hard drive or a secure, encrypted cloud service. Cloud platforms such as Google Drive, Dropbox, or OneDrive work well—just make sure to enable **two-factor authentication** for added protection.

When naming your digital files, keep labels simple and consistent—for example, *LastWill_JohnSmith_2024.pdf* or *POA_MarySmith_2023.pdf.* Create main folders that match the sections of your physical binder: **Legal, Finance, Insurance, Health, Property, Contacts,** and **Personal.** Avoid generic file names or dumping everything into one folder. Clear, logical organization saves time and prevents confusion when someone else needs to locate documents quickly.

Always password-protect any folders or drives containing sensitive files. Consider using a password manager to store combinations securely and share access with only the most trusted individuals. Besides storing in the cloud, keep a backup copy on a separate, encrypted external drive. If the house suffers a disaster, digital backups can ensure nothing gets lost. Periodically check your backups to make certain everything works properly and stays up to date.

Sensitive papers need both protection from outsiders and immediate access for loved ones in case of an emergency. Avoid hiding document binders or encrypted files so well that even responsible family members cannot locate them under pressure. For the physical binder, show at least one trusted person where it is and how to open any locks. For digital storage, share clear written instructions (and necessary passwords) either in person, in a sealed envelope, or through your attorney.

A thoughtful organization method means you do more than gather papers—you set family members up to succeed when the time comes. Passing along the secret location of your binder, a shared drive, or handoff instructions gives those you trust the real gift: the ability to act swiftly on your behalf, without stumbling through guesswork. Ensuring access is the natural next step to making your organizational efforts truly helpful and lasting.

Sharing Access with Key People

A carefully organized folder, binder, or digital file only provides real protection for your loved ones if people know exactly where to find these documents. Many families keep their will, power of attorney, or healthcare directives locked away, only to discover in a crisis that nobody knows the location or how to access them. When you organize your estate documents, the next step is thinking about who will need to find them quickly in times of illness, incapacity, or after your passing.

Imagine a scenario where an adult child needs a parent's will to start probate but cannot even find the right drawer. Or a power of attorney document sits encrypted on a laptop, with the password long forgotten. This happens more often than many expect, leading to expensive legal delays, locked bank accounts, or confusion at the hospital. Families left without guidance often feel lost and sometimes need a court's permission to take basic steps. On the other hand, when people receive clear directions—such as a spouse shown exactly where documents are and how to access digital files—they resolve matters quickly and privately.

Being selective about who can find and use your estate planning documents keeps your information safe while ensuring someone trustworthy is always prepared. Most people choose a spouse, adult child, or executor. Others involve a trusted friend or financial advisor. The important thing is not to give everyone access but to think through who genuinely needs it. This keeps your plan private, shields your documents from outsiders, and protects your legacy from unnecessary eyes.

Start by making a short, clear list of the individuals who should know about your estate documents. Consider their reliability, location, and your comfort level. Then, decide the best way to share information securely.

Ways to Communicate Document Locations

Face-to-Face Conversation

- Invite the person to a private space.
- Explain what documents you have and where you store them.
- If there are keys or combination codes involved, show them how to access these.
- Walk through the process together if possible.

Written Instructions

- Write a simple, clear note outlining each document's name and storage location.
- List any steps needed (for example, "key to box is in kitchen drawer").

- Place this note in a secure spot, such as a safe deposit box or family safe.
- Tell your trusted individual how to find the note.

Family or Executor Meeting

- Gather only those who genuinely need this information.
- Share general details—what exists and who can access it—without revealing passwords or private legal details in front of everyone.
- Allow time for questions so there is no remaining uncertainty.

Sharing Digital Access Safely

Digital asset management is more common with wills or financial documents stored on computers or in cloud folders. The risk comes if a password, security question, or device lockout keeps your team from retrieving what's needed.

- Keep a password list in a locked safe or safe deposit box. Update it when you change passwords.
- Use a password management tool with shared access features. Many offer the ability to add a trusted emergency contact.
- Prepare sealed envelopes containing access instructions to be given to your attorney or executor. The envelope stays shut until needed.
- Never email passwords or sensitive information, as messages can be intercepted or accounts hacked.

Example of a Clear Password Sharing Process

1. Write or print a list of passwords for all devices and key accounts.
2. Place the list in a sealed envelope.
3. Store the envelope in a fireproof safe.
4. Give your chosen person instructions on where to find the envelope and when to use it.
5. Check every six to twelve months that the passwords are still current.

Protecting Privacy and Security

Share information only through safe, controlled means. Refrain from sending storage details by text or email. Communicate sensitive details only by secure phone call, trusted written note, or in person.

Make it easy for your trusted helper to report changes, lost keys, or a forgotten password. Whenever you move documents or update passwords, let the right people know as soon as possible. Schedule check-ins or short meetings if circumstances change or a review feels necessary. Encourage your helpers to ask questions if they are unclear what steps to take.

Written instructions offer reassurance that no step will be forgotten. Keep them simple, and make sure they are available when needed. At the same time, store them where only the appropriate person can access them to avoid theft or tampering.

Building a routine for sharing updates and open communication with your trusted contacts means your estate plan will stay accurate as your life changes. Regular touchpoints with your key people make it much easier to keep everything up to date, supporting the full intent behind your careful organization. This clear chain of access equips your family with confidence, saves time, and reduces legal headaches when the unexpected occurs.

Setting Calendar Reminders for Regular Updates

Staying on top of estate planning requires more than building trust and sharing information with loved ones. Even after decisions are made and documents are in order, estate planning should be treated as an ongoing responsibility. Life continually evolves—new family members arrive, finances shift, and health circumstances change. Without regular reviews and timely updates, an estate plan can easily fall out of step with reality. Outdated information or overlooked details may lead to confusion, legal delays, and extra costs at the very moment when clarity matters most. Loved ones may struggle to carry out your wishes if they aren't clearly or fully expressed.

Regular review is the best way to keep an estate plan current and effective. Scheduling a yearly check-in helps everything stay organized and up to date. Tying your review to a familiar annual milestone works well—many people choose tax season, the start of summer, a birthday, or the beginning of the school year. Linking the task to a recurring event turns it into a habit rather than a chore. For example, you might decide to revisit your estate plan each spring after filing taxes. This approach keeps the process simple, structured, and less likely to be forgotten.

Sudden life events can also signal the need for immediate updates. After a marriage, divorce, the birth of a child or grandchild, a major purchase such as a new home, a significant health change, or the loss of a loved one, take time to ensure your plan still reflects your current reality. Here are some examples to keep in mind:

- Getting married or divorced can mean changing or adding beneficiaries.
- Having a baby or grandchild might call for an update to the will or trust.
- Moving to a new home means updating property records and addresses.

- Opening or closing accounts requires checking that ownership and beneficiaries are current.
- Serious health changes may prompt you to revisit powers of attorney or healthcare directives.

To make these good intentions stick, reminders are crucial. Digital calendars make it easy to set recurring annual alerts. In Google Calendar or Outlook, add a new event for "Estate Plan Review," set the date to your chosen milestone, and select "repeat yearly." Set a phone alarm for the same day to have an extra nudge. If you prefer physical reminders, write the review date on a family wall calendar or your planner. Marking the date in a visible spot puts the task front and center—as likely to be noticed as any family birthday. People less comfortable with digital tools can follow these simple steps:

1. Pick a regular event or fixed date (for example, April 15).
2. On a smartphone, open the calendar app and tap the date.
3. Add an event titled "Estate Plan Review."
4. Set the event to repeat each year.
5. Select a notification alert—many phones let you get a reminder a day ahead.
6. Also, write the date on your home calendar or planner for backup.

Alongside reminders, a quick checklist for maintaining an estate plan can bring order to the process. Place this checklist right inside your estate planning folder or save it in the same digital location as your documents. A typical checklist might look like this:

- Check beneficiary designations for all life insurance, retirement, and investment accounts
- Review will instructions and asset lists
- Confirm powers of attorney for finances and healthcare reflect current wishes
- Update healthcare directives as needed

- Review account titles and ownership for new or closed accounts
- Confirm contact lists for lawyers, financial advisors, and emergency contacts are up-to-date

Reviewing these items annually ensures accuracy and readiness for future requirements.

Documenting each review and change is valuable for both clarity and peace of mind. On the first page of each estate document, write the review date by hand or add a note to the digital file. For major changes, keep a short change log or summary sheet in the same folder, listing the date and reason for each update. For example, write: "June 5, 2024—Changed primary residence address after moving." Keeping these notes makes it easy for family or professionals to follow your decisions and understand your intentions.

A well-maintained estate plan serves as a steady safety net for family and friends. It protects not only property but also relationships, avoiding conflict and confusion during already stressful times. Taking just a little time each year to review, update, and record changes creates lasting reassurance that your wishes will be understood and honored when the time comes.

Bringing It All Together

Now that you understand the importance of organizing, storing, sharing, and regularly updating your estate planning documents, you can take confident steps to secure your family's future. By creating an accessible estate binder, backing up digital copies, and clearly communicating access with trusted individuals, you reduce confusion and costly delays when your plan is needed most. Setting calendar reminders for annual reviews and promptly updating changes ensures your wishes remain current and clear over time. This careful preparation protects your assets and provides peace of mind, knowing your loved ones have the guidance they need to carry out your intentions smoothly and without unnecessary stress.

CHAPTER 12

UPDATING YOUR ESTATE PLAN AS LIFE CHANGES

Have you ever made an important plan, only to have life change in ways you didn't expect? Maybe you got married, had a child, or experienced a shift in your finances. How confident are you that the plan you created still fits your current situation? Many people put time into making an estate plan, but few realize how often it needs to be reviewed and updated. What happens if you forget to adjust your wishes after significant changes occur? Could outdated documents cause confusion or unintended consequences for those you care about most? These are common concerns that many face but seldom prepare for. Understanding when and why to revisit your estate plan is key to making sure it accurately reflects your life today —and the future you want to protect.

Key Moments to Update and Edit Your Estate Plan

Significant changes in life often mean it is time to look over your estate plan. Careful updates make sure your wishes are clearly carried out and your loved ones are protected. Missing a review can create confusion, legal trouble, and heartbreak in times that are already stressful. Many people don't realize just how many types of events can affect an estate plan's integrity.

Marriage or Divorce

Marriage typically means you want your spouse to be taken care of. If your will or beneficiary forms don't mention your new spouse, they might not inherit anything directly, or an ex-spouse could remain the main beneficiary. This situation becomes more complicated in blended families with children from previous relationships. During a divorce, if you forget to remove your former spouse from documents, they might still receive life insurance benefits, act as your healthcare agent, or inherit everything you leave behind.

Real-world example

Imagine someone names their spouse as the sole beneficiary of their retirement account. Years later, they divorce, but never update the beneficiary. If that person dies, the ex-spouse may still receive the full account, even if the person has remarried. Courts often uphold the named beneficiary, regardless of personal wishes or the current marriage.

New Children and Changing Family Structures

When a child is born or adopted, a review is in order. If you do not add the new child or update guardianship appointments, that child could be left with nothing or be without a clear guardian if both parents pass away. Families also shift when adult children become old enough to take on responsibilities. They may need to be added as agents for power of attorney or trusted representatives in case you're unable to make your own decisions.

What Can Go Wrong

Suppose your will was drafted before your youngest child was born. If nothing changes, only your older children may inherit, while your youngest is left out. Or maybe you have health care directives that name your brother as your agent, but now your adult daughter is better suited for the job.

Significant Changes in Financial Status

Financial ups and downs matter too. Inheriting a large sum, getting a major job bonus, or selling a business can all reshape your plan. If these gains and losses aren't reflected in your instructions, your plan might not divide wealth as you want. Taxes on inheritance or gifts given during life can also be different, so updating may help your family avoid big bills.

Example

If your estate plan was built around a house and modest savings, but then you launch a successful business, that business needs to be considered. Mishandling business succession can trigger family arguments, or tax headaches that drain the value of your hard work.

Becoming a Caregiver or Needing Care

Taking care of aging parents, or if you develop health concerns, means plans should list divorce but your bank accounts or health decisions. Appointing powers of attorney or updating advance directives lets people step in at the right time with the legal authority to make choices. If too many documents exist with different names, or if outdated forms forget new helpers, it can cause power struggles or gaps in care.

The Risks of Not Making Official, Legal Updates

Handwritten changes in the margins, crossing out names, or making promises aloud aren't enough. These attempts often get challenged and usually fail in court. Each state has rules about signatures, witnesses, and what makes a document valid. Skipping any step can mean your plan isn't followed, period.

Working with Professionals

Even if you use an online service to fill out forms, it's smart to check with an estate planning attorney. They double-check that everything fits together, follows current laws, and closes any loopholes. A professional also spots issues like outdated beneficiary forms for retirement accounts or insurance policies, which aren't controlled by your will or trust. These forms need their own review and updates, or old choices can override your intentions.

Staying Organized and Proactive

Set annual or biannual reminders to review your full set of documents. Create a checklist for each life event:

- Will and trusts
- Beneficiary designations for retirement, investment, and insurance accounts
- Power of attorney and health care directives
- Guardianship nominations

Compare each form to your real-life relationships and finances. Make sure every name, amount, and responsibility is accurate, with no old contacts left over.

What Happens When Updates Are Neglected

Skipping a review can mean a special needs child is left without support, or adult children fight in court over medical decisions. Loved ones might have to endure drawn-out probate battles, or face large taxes that could have been avoided.

Life keeps moving, but laws and technology around estate planning change too. Being alert to these shifts means your wishes stay current and safe regardless of future developments.

Adapting to Legal and Technological Changes

Estate planning requires close attention when major life events call for quick action—but those moments are only part of the bigger picture. Life keeps moving, and so do the laws and tools that shape how an estate plan functions in practice. Keeping everything up to date means staying alert to legal changes and new strategies that might alter what's possible—or even disrupt arrangements you put in place years ago. The plans designed to protect your family's future need ongoing care, not just a one-time signature.

Estate laws can change at both the federal and state levels, sometimes in ways that surprise even experienced planners. After a marriage, divorce, the birth of a child, or a financial shift, it's natural to update your documents. But what happens when Congress lowers the federal estate tax exemption? If the amount of wealth you can pass on tax-free decreases, your plan might unintentionally expose heirs to new taxes. State governments also adjust regulations for items like health care directives and powers of attorney. A document that was valid three years ago might no longer meet current standards. For instance, if your state tightens the signing requirements for a living will, your document could be ruled invalid—and your wishes ignored as a result.

The details of beneficiary designations also come under scrutiny in changing legal environments. Sometimes, rules about who can inherit retirement accounts shift, or states introduce new forms for registering transfer-on-death designations. If you're not watching these changes, you could unintentionally disinherit a loved one or make the asset transfer process longer and costlier for your family.

The most powerful step in staying current is to take an active role in monitoring legal developments that affect estate planning. Reliable information can be found through official state government websites and the Internal Revenue Service for federal tax laws. Estate planning organizations often produce plain-language updates about changes in statutes or case law. Many attorneys' offices issue timely legal bulletins or offer summaries following major policy updates. Monitoring these sources can assist you in identifying significant changes that could impact your plan.

Professional help adds another layer of security and comfort. Law and policy updates can be confusing, which makes regular contact with an estate planning attorney or financial advisor very helpful. Scheduling an annual or biannual document review takes only a small amount of time, and in return, you receive peace of mind that your plan remains effective and legally sound. Some professionals offer email newsletters; subscribing connects you to timely alerts about the latest developments. Examples include your attorney reviewing your trust after state tax laws shift or your advisor helping you see what new retirement account rules mean for your intended heirs. These relationships offer both day-to-day support and deep guidance when large-scale legal changes occur.

Technology brings welcome simplicity and speed to estate planning. New tools can help you keep your documents secure, up-to-date, and easily accessible to those who need them. Secure online document vaults store digital copies of your most important paperwork, from wills to powers of attorney, and let you grant access to trusted family members or advisors. Encryption keeps your sensitive information safe, while cloud storage makes it possible to update forms without waiting for meetings or mailing paperwork.

Asset inventory apps let you record valuables, accounts, and digital assets—all in one place.

Online platforms simplify communication with professionals and loved ones. Instead of mailing forms or scheduling in-person signings each time there's a small change, you can use digital signature tools or secure portals to share updates fast. With more wealth held in digital accounts and even cryptocurrencies, planning for so-called "digital assets" has become vital. Having a clear process for passing on email, financial accounts, or cryptocurrency keys prevents loss and confusion for your heirs.

Some actionable steps help keep your estate plan on track in a changing world:

- Keep a recurring checklist to review plan documents in light of new legal or tax conditions each year.
- Organize your estate documents in both digital and paper versions, storing each securely and keeping track of who has access.
- Sign up for legal update emails from attorneys, estate planning organizations, and trusted financial sources.
- Use online portals or secure messaging to communicate changes with multiple professionals at once.
- After tax law changes, update your will or trust as soon as possible, even if you only need to adjust a few details.

Staying alert and making use of professional advice, supported by good digital tools, is the simplest way to keep your plan effective into the future. Active care protects your loved ones from surprises and hassle. Establishing the habit of reviewing, discussing, and refining your plans regularly turns estate management into a protective tradition that can support your family across generations.

Making Estate Planning a Lifelong Habit

After looking at the big forces—like changing laws and evolving technology—that can affect estate planning, it becomes clear that building regular review habits matters just as much. Treating estate planning as a single event feels natural in the beginning. People check the boxes, sign the documents, and set them aside. Later, this can cause trouble for families who realize too late that things have drifted out of date. Over time, it is quiet, steady attention that preserves both intentions and peace of mind.

Small steps done every year take less effort than major overhauls, and they help the plan stay reliable as life changes. One simple trick is to put an annual reminder on a phone or digital calendar. This prompt gives a nudge to pull out estate documents and double-check important details. Instead of feeling overwhelmed, readers can set aside just an afternoon to look over beneficiary designations, will instructions, or any healthcare directives. Digital tools, like reminder apps and calendar scheduling, make this habit almost automatic. Someone who receives an alert every January will remember to look for errors, outgrown appointments, or family changes reflected in their paperwork.

Pairing this annual review with a personal milestone can help it feel more natural instead of forced. Marking birthdays, anniversaries, or even tax season as moments to glance at estate materials gives the routine a built-in cue. For example, one family decided that each year during tax filing, they would also check that their children's guardianship arrangements and account lists were still right. Another person set up a calendar invite for her birthday so she could look over her documents while also celebrating how much had changed in her life since the previous year. For many, these seasonal reminders keep the topic from becoming forgotten or overwhelming.

Estate planning is not just about paperwork—it's about people. Encouraging open communication within the family makes a meaningful difference. Holding regular family meetings, even once a year, helps everyone stay aligned on wishes, roles, and expectations. It's best to keep these conversations structured but simple. Topics might include reviewing account changes, welcoming new family members through marriage or birth, or noting any health concerns.

Starting these discussions can feel uncomfortable at first. Some families find it easier to begin with gratitude—saying something like, *"I want to thank everyone for helping make sure our plans stay current."* Others break the ice by referencing a real-life example, such as a news story about estate confusion after someone's passing. Using outside examples or appreciation can help shift the tone from tense to cooperative.

Sharing responsibility among family members also strengthens the process. Instead of one person managing everything, divide tasks so each person handles a specific part—like tracking health updates, keeping a digital asset list, or maintaining a secure folder of documents. One family found success by assigning one member to oversee health records, another to organize account passwords, and a third to maintain the estate binder. With each person holding a manageable piece, no one feels overwhelmed, and important details receive consistent attention. Delegating in this way builds trust and ensures that essential knowledge isn't lost if someone becomes unavailable.

Keeping a clear, updated **checklist** brings order to even the most complicated life changes. Beyond wills and powers of attorney, include digital assets such as email accounts, cloud storage, social media logins, streaming services, and even phone passcodes. If no one can find these details when needed, frustration and wasted time often follow. For instance, one widow spent weeks trying to access her late husband's email, only to discover the password had been discarded with a sticky note. Another family used a shared password manager, keeping every update in sync—making transitions simple and stress-free for everyone involved.

A proactive approach to estate planning offers quiet benefits that surface during life's most challenging times. Relatives feel less stress when they already know where to look and whom to ask for information. Family members understand their responsibilities, wishes get carried out more clearly, and even small moments of reflection reinforce bonds. An up-to-date plan helps prevent fights or confusion, which often come from surprises hidden in old paperwork.

Routine review of an estate plan deserves a spot alongside annual finances and health checkups. This is not only about paperwork or savings but also about family stability and peace of mind. Turning maintenance into a habit means that loved ones will face fewer obstacles, smoother transitions, and a lasting legacy that really fits readers' true wishes. Making the time each year to review and communicate provides everyone a stronger sense of security—something that no single, one-time effort can provide.

Concluding Thoughts

Now that we understand the many life changes and legal shifts that can impact an estate plan, it is clear that regular updates are not optional but essential. By making a habit of reviewing and adjusting your documents annually or after major events, you ensure your wishes remain accurate and legally sound. This ongoing attentiveness protects your family from confusion, costly disputes, and unexpected tax burdens. Embracing a proactive approach, with help from professionals when needed, turns estate planning into a manageable routine that secures your legacy and provides lasting peace of mind for you and those you care about most.

YOUR VOICE CAN PROTECT SOMEONE'S LEGACY

Every plan we create today can become a **gift of clarity** for someone tomorrow.

Have you thought about what would happen to your family if you weren't there to help?

Picture a grieving family—already overwhelmed—trying to navigate courts, paperwork, and financial confusion because no clear estate plan was left behind. Your reflections on ***Estate Planning*** could give future readers the reassurance and direction they need to avoid this painful scenario.

If this book helped you *understand the essentials*, *organize your assets more clearly*, or *take the first steps toward protecting your family*, I'd be truly honored if you would leave a short, honest review.

Your feedback not only supports my work—it also becomes a **beacon** for readers who may be standing right where you once stood: *uncertain, hesitant, but ready to protect what matters most.* Even a few sentences can ripple outward, helping others find the tools and courage to prepare for their future.

Thank you for reading, reflecting, and sharing your journey. **Your words carry more power than you may realize.**

CONCLUSION

You've taken important steps on a journey that, for many people, feels overwhelming before it even begins. By creating an estate plan—one tailored to your life and the people you love—you've not only secured peace of mind for yourself but also provided protection and clarity for those dearest to you. The confidence that comes from knowing your wishes are clear and your future provisions are in place is no small accomplishment. As you reach the end of this process, recognize the gift you've created: stability, certainty, and care, all delivered with intention and love.

Throughout this book, we explored the key components of an effective estate plan, breaking down what often feels complicated into manageable, actionable steps. We began by showing that estate planning isn't only for the wealthy or the elderly—it's a practical act of care for anyone who has assets, responsibilities, or loved ones they wish to protect. Whether you're in your thirties and beginning to build wealth, a parent focused on your children's security, a homeowner hoping to avoid probate delays, or someone caring for aging relatives, your circumstances make estate planning both relevant and necessary.

At the heart of every estate plan are the core documents that form its foundation. A **will** ensures that your property and belongings are distributed according to your wishes, preventing confusion and disputes among family members. **Powers of attorney**—for both finances and healthcare—place trusted individuals in charge if you ever become unable to make decisions yourself. **Health care directives** outline the treatments you want or wish to avoid, sparing loved ones from making painful choices in emotional moments. **Living trusts** can provide privacy, shorten probate, and reduce the risk of legal challenges. When these documents are clear, current, and well organized, they can turn what might be a stressful transition into a smooth and confident one for your family.

Equally important are the decisions you've already started making throughout this process. You identified who you trust to carry out your wishes, thoughtfully considered guardianship for your children or dependents, and clarified your intentions regarding health care and financial matters. For homeowners, you assessed how your property would transfer, possibly avoiding lengthy court proceedings. If you have special accounts, insurance policies, or retirement plans, you updated beneficiaries so everything aligns seamlessly. Each choice was a step toward relieving future burdens and ensuring your legacy is preserved with integrity.

Many readers begin this book feeling unsure where to start or anxious about making mistakes. That's understandable. Legal language can be intimidating, and the thought of sitting down to consider end-of-life scenarios is rarely appealing. But you have seen that planning is not an all-or-nothing task. Each piece fits together over time, at your pace. Remember, perfection is not required—progress is what truly matters. Even imperfect plans, updated as your life evolves, make an enormous difference compared to having no plan at all.

If you ever find yourself hesitating, remember that estate planning is a living process. You can begin today by putting just one document in place—even something as simple as drafting a basic will or naming a power of attorney. As life evolves, revisit your plan periodically. Adjustments are not only natural, they're wise. Milestones such as marriage, divorce, the birth of a child, or changes in your financial situation all call for thoughtful updates. No matter your age or stage in life, now is always the right time to begin.

It's also natural to have questions or face unique circumstances. Seeking guidance is a sign of strength, not uncertainty. Many people choose to consult a qualified attorney for complex estates, blended families, business ownership, or other special considerations. With today's wide range of online tools and affordable planning software, you can also begin the process independently—reviewing drafts and options at your own pace before deciding whether professional input is needed. Whichever path you choose, include your family in the conversation. Open communication prevents misunderstanding and reinforces the true purpose of your planning: to care for the people you love.

Leaving a legacy isn't defined by the size of your bank account or the number of properties you own. It's about preserving your values, protecting those closest to you, and minimizing unnecessary cost and stress. Estate planning gives your family the freedom to focus on healing and supporting one another instead of struggling through confusion and paperwork. The stories you share, the memories you pass on, and the thoughtful instructions you leave behind are among the most meaningful gifts you can offer.

Consider the peace that comes from having a plan in hand. Your loved ones are spared guesswork. Vital information is accessible when needed most. Bills get paid, homes are protected, and cherished possessions find their way to the people who will value them most. With the steps you have taken—and those you continue to take—you affirm that your wishes matter and that those who count on you will be cared for, no matter what. This is your legacy, shaped by your decisions and grounded in your intention.

It's natural to still wonder if you've done enough or if your plan will stand the test of time. Rest assured, the effort you have invested will make a lasting impact. While laws may change and your life may shift; foundational steps—updating documents, communicating wishes, and selecting trustworthy representatives—will always be relevant. Regular reviews ensure that your plan remains current. Most importantly, your loved ones will understand that they were your top priority at every stage.

Now is the moment to celebrate both the clarity you've created and the empowerment you feel. You haven't just checked off a legal requirement; you've claimed control over your future and given your family a roadmap for navigating life's transitions. Let this accomplishment spur you forward. If there are still pieces left unfinished, return to them with renewed confidence. If you're ready to take the next step, reach out for expert help or leverage technology to fine-tune your plan. If the hardest part—a conversation about the future—awaits, open the dialogue with honesty and care.

Take pride in what you've achieved. You've built something priceless: a safety net for those you love most, designed on your terms. Every page turned, every decision made, has moved you closer to lasting peace of mind. Let this mark the beginning—not the end—of living with greater assurance, knowing your legacy will endure through whatever tomorrow may bring.

PART TWO
LIVING TRUSTS

HOW TO SET UP A LIVING TRUST, PROTECT YOUR ASSETS, BYPASS PROBATE, SAVE BIG ON TAXES, AND SECURE YOUR FAMILY'S FUTURE WITHOUT EXPENSIVE LAWYERS OR COMPLICATED PAPERWORK

INTRODUCTION

Imagine a moment, years from now, when your family gathers to reflect on the life you built and the legacy you leave behind. In that quiet room, emotions run high—because loss always brings pain—but there's something else: clarity, order, and peace of mind. There are no frantic searches for paperwork, no marathon meetings with lawyers, and no endless waiting for courts to decide what happens next. Instead, your wishes are honored swiftly and smoothly. Assets move seamlessly to loved ones. The home you worked hard for remains in the family. Children and grandchildren receive their inheritance without strife or expense. There's relief at a time when it matters most. This future isn't just possible—it's closer than you think. And it starts with a simple document: the living trust.

Maybe you've heard about living trusts before or skimmed articles online. Perhaps a friend mentioned them in passing, or a financial advisor dropped the term into conversation. But if you're like millions of Americans, the world of estate planning still feels confusing and intimidating. Legal terms blur together. Probate sounds mysterious—something that only happens to other people, until it doesn't. It's not surprising: for decades, estate planning has been shrouded in jargon and treated as a luxury reserved for the wealthy. As a result, many middle-class families, regular homeowners, and well-intentioned parents delay planning, uncertain about where to start or how much it will cost.

The truth is, most people misunderstand what a living trust actually is. Some think it's only for the rich or those with complex business empires. Some think it's like a will or that it means giving up control of assets early. These myths persist because professional advice too often comes wrapped in complexity—with expensive hourly fees and intimidating forms. Yet a living trust is not a privilege of the wealthy, nor is it an instrument that takes away your autonomy. In its essence, a living trust is a legal arrangement that allows you to transfer ownership of your property, investments, and other assets into a trust that you control while you're alive. You can change or revoke it at any time. When you pass away, the successor you named steps in and distributes your assets directly to the people you care about most—bypassing costly court proceedings and minimizing potential disputes.

Why does this matter so much? Because failing to plan means leaving your legacy in the hands of strangers—judges, lawyers, and government officials who don't know your family or your intentions. Without a living trust, your loved ones will likely face probate, an expensive, public, and time-consuming court process required to validate your will and oversee the distribution of your assets. Probate is a roadblock at a time of grief. It routinely takes six months to a year—or longer—before heirs gain access to property and funds. Meanwhile, legal fees and administrative expenses can eat up five percent or more of your estate. Even simple estates aren't immune. Homes may need to be sold under pressure. Bank accounts can be frozen. Family businesses risk disruption or dissolution. Sibling disputes and blended family complications sometimes escalate into lasting rifts. Every year, court costs and legal battles divert billions of dollars intended for families due to a lack of timely planning.

A living trust may be the single most important document you ever create if you own a home, have children or grandchildren, or want to spare your loved ones unnecessary hardship. Unlike a standard will—which guarantees probate—a living trust ensures your legacy is handled privately, efficiently, and in line with your exact wishes. You retain full control of your assets throughout your life, with the freedom to buy, sell, refinance, or make changes whenever you choose. When the unexpected happens, your instructions remain clear, avoiding confusion and chaos for those left behind. For parents and grandparents, this means protecting children's inheritances until they are mature enough to handle them responsibly. For business owners, it means providing for uninterrupted leadership and the smooth transition of key assets. For those caring for aging parents, it offers a way to provide ongoing support, even if mental capacity diminishes. In blended families, it delivers clarity, equity, and fairness that everyone understands.

So why do so few people take this vital step? Fear and uncertainty often dominate the answer. The idea of confronting our mortality is daunting. The prospect of wading through legal paperwork is overwhelming, especially when so much is at stake. Many people fear making mistakes or falling victim to unethical advisors. Worst of all, some delay estate planning entirely—hoping that "one day" will suffice. Yet every day, ordinary families pay the price for that hesitation.

The good news is that setting up a living trust is far simpler and more affordable than you might imagine. With the right roadmap, you don't need a law degree—or even a lawyer—to put one in place. This book was written for individuals and families just like you: adults navigating the responsibilities of homeownership, parenthood, caregiving, or entrepreneurship; people who want clarity without complexity; and do-it-yourselfers who value actionable guidance over legalese. Inside, you'll find step-by-step instructions tailored for real life, using plain language and practical tools. I'll walk you through every stage of the process, from deciding whether a living trust makes sense for your circumstances to drafting key documents, funding your trust, and ensuring your wishes hold up over time. You'll learn how to avoid common pitfalls, sidestep needless expenses, and secure peace of mind for yourself and those you love most.

There's no sugarcoating the significance of these decisions or the comfort that comes from knowing your affairs are in order. A living trust is more than a legal document: it's a powerful act of love and responsibility. By taking action now, you dramatically simplify the path for your family during their most vulnerable moments. You eliminate barriers, preserve hard-earned assets, and shield your loved ones from bureaucratic headaches and emotional strain. Most importantly, you ensure the legacy you built endures long after you're gone—not just in material wealth, but in the security, dignity, and stability you provide.

Throughout the pages ahead, I'll demystify every facet of living trusts and estate planning, revealing options that fit a wide spectrum of needs—from modest homes to growing small businesses, from young professionals starting out to retirees looking for lasting security. Whether you're preparing for your own later years or helping a parent, partner, or adult child, you'll find the confidence to act and the knowledge to get it done right.

Your journey to a stronger legacy begins here. Let's remove the uncertainty, reduce the burden, and make sure your final gift to your loved ones is a future free from needless obstacles. No lawyer required—just the willingness to start today.

CHAPTER 13
LIVING TRUST BASICS—WHAT YOU NEED TO KNOW BEFORE YOU START

Years ago, when my parents first began sorting through their estate plans, the complexity and uncertainty felt overwhelming. Terms like "trustee," "probate," and "beneficiary" were tossed around with little explanation, leaving important decisions tangled in confusion and delay. Watching their experience unfold revealed how common misunderstandings about living trusts often stand between families and smooth transitions.

Understanding the basics of living trusts—their purpose, key terms, how they differ from wills, and the real benefits they provide—can simplify a process that many find intimidating. This chapter lays the foundation for making informed choices by breaking down what living trusts are, why they matter, and how they help protect both your assets and your family's future.

Understanding Living Trusts and Essential Terms

A living trust is a legal tool that helps people manage and pass on their property without court delays or public involvement. It allows someone to put their assets, like homes or accounts, into a trust while alive so that after death, these assets move directly to the people chosen as beneficiaries. In basic terms, a living trust works like a special container. Instead of owning assets in your own name, you hold them through the trust. You set the rules, pick who manages everything, and decide who gets what when you die or become unable to handle things on your own.

Understanding the differences between a living trust and a will helps make things clearer. Both transfer assets to loved ones, but they do it in different ways. A will only goes into effect after you die. The will must go to probate court, which is a public legal process where a judge makes sure your instructions are followed. This can take months, and anyone can look up your will in public records. A living trust, by contrast, takes effect as soon as you sign and fund it. If you are alive but can't handle your affairs—say, because you're sick or injured—the trust lets someone else step in automatically. After your death, there is no probate for assets in the trust. Family members do not have to wait for court approval, and the process stays private.

Think of two common family examples. Joe and Rita, homeowners with grown children, have a will that names the kids as heirs. When Joe passes, everything owned in his name hits probate, even the house. The children have to wait until the judge approves the will and transfers the home. Rosie, instead, uses a living trust and puts the house and bank accounts in it while alive. Her children do not need court help. The successor trustee handles the paperwork, and her kids get the house smoothly.

Breaking down key terms builds confidence in handling these choices. A trust is a legal agreement where you give someone responsibility to manage what you own for another person's benefit. The living trust is a trust you set up while you are alive—meaning not in your will and not after your death. Most living trusts are revocable trusts, which means you can change or cancel the trust any time while you are alive and mentally alert. If you buy a new home or change your mind about who gets what, you don't need to start over.

The person who creates the trust is the grantor. Other common terms for this role are "settlor" or "trustor"—all mean the same person, the one putting property into the trust. The grantor keeps control if they name themselves as the initial trustee, which is very common. The trustee is the individual or company responsible for handling the trust according to your written instructions. If you are able, you serve as a trustee for your living trust. If something happens to you, the person you choose as successor trustee takes over management. This person follows your instructions, pays bills, handles final debts, and then gives out assets as you planned. The beneficiary is the person or group who receives the property or money from the trust, such as a spouse, children, grandchildren, or charity.

Imagine Alice, who owns a house and savings account. She makes a living trust, names herself as trustee, and moves her home and accounts into the trust's name. She names her daughter as a successor trustee and both of her children as beneficiaries. If Alice becomes sick and can't manage bills, her daughter starts acting as trustee right away. After Alice's death, her daughter follows the instructions: pays leftover bills and then gives the house to the brother and sister.

Common property that goes into living trusts includes real estate—like homes or cottages—bank accounts, savings, investment accounts, stocks, bonds, and valuable personal possessions. Some items, such as retirement accounts or life insurance, already pass directly through named beneficiaries, so they are not usually moved into the trust. A will is still useful if you want to name a guardian for minor children, or to transfer items not placed into the trust, such as a car or family heirlooms you did not retitle.

Making these choices gives practical benefits beyond just passing property. Living trusts offer privacy for the family, since there are no public court records. They also mean that managing or distributing assets does not have to wait for the courts, saving time and stress. This stronger control and privacy helps families take care of loved ones more smoothly, even when life takes an unexpected turn or health changes quickly. Now that the basics are clear, it becomes possible to see why setting up a living trust may be worth considering and how these benefits can make a difference for real families.

Exploring the Key Benefits of Living Trusts

Families often discover the true difference between a **will** and a **living trust** during difficult times—not when these documents are first created. While a will serves a clear and essential purpose, it also requires involvement with the probate court system. A living trust helps bypass that process, allowing you to transfer property privately, efficiently, and with greater control. Understanding how each tool functions gives you a real advantage when deciding what's best for the people you love.

Privacy: Keeping Family Matters Out of the Public Eye

Wills must go through probate court, which is an open, public process. Anyone can check court records and learn what assets are in an estate, who gets them, and even see disputes between family members. With a living trust, the details remain private. The only people who need to know are your chosen trustees and beneficiaries.

Picture a mother named Linda, whose wish is to leave her home and savings to her children after she dies. If she leaves these assets in a will, they become part of a public record, easily searchable in probate filings. Friends, neighbors, and even scam artists could see exactly what Linda owned and who inherited it. With a living trust, Linda's personal information and family details do not leave the living room. Only those named in the trust know how the inheritance is divided. Many people worry that complete privacy sounds unrealistic, especially in the digital age. In reality, a properly set up living trust offers a solid layer of protection from prying eyes.

Probate Avoidance: Faster, Simpler, and Less Stressful

Probate is more than just a word lawyers throw around. It is the legal process where the court reviews a will, deals with debts, and approves the distribution of assets. This takes months or even longer, often a year or more. In the meantime, family members may not have access to funds needed to pay bills, handle repairs, or settle urgent financial needs. They may also be required to attend multiple court dates, and the court may hold up asset transfers for reasons outside their control.

When a property is owned by a living trust, the probate process is skipped entirely. The assets are distributed by the person you choose, called your trustee, according to the rules set up in the trust. If a homeowner named Samuel places his house in a living trust, his spouse or children can take care of paperwork and transfer the title within weeks—not months or years. This is a relief for many, since grieving families are already facing enough pressure. A frequent worry is whether the trust will actually do what it promises—that is, let people avoid probate delays. The reality is, assuming the trust is funded (the assets are formally transferred into it), there are no courts involved and no waiting for a judge's approval.

Typical Timeline: Probate vs. Living Trust

- **Probate with a Will:** 6–18 months (possible court fees, delays, and paperwork)
- **Living Trust Distribution:** Usually 1–4 weeks (direct by trustee, minimal court involvement)

Personal Control: Deciding How and When Assets Are Shared

Wills usually leave assets all at once, so an 18-year-old might suddenly inherit a large sum, ready or not. Living trusts let you set clear conditions and schedules. You can give a portion of money when a child turns 21, another at 25, or tie later gifts to finishing college.

Imagine a parent, Roberta, who wants to help her teenage children but also wants to prevent misuse or waste. In her living trust, she can state that her son receives money every year for living expenses, but larger amounts are only released when certain life goals are met. A blended family, say two remarried parents with kids from earlier marriages, may want to be sure both their biological and stepchildren receive what is fair. With a trust, you write these instructions in detail, preventing confusion or future disagreement. Some people fear that such rules become too rigid or get ignored. As long as you name a responsible trustee and update the trust if life changes, your plan will be honored and enforced in the way you intend.

Why These Benefits Matter

Privacy allows families to avoid unwanted attention, embarrassment, or outside interference. **Bypassing probate** saves months of time, legal fees, and emotional strain when loved ones are already coping with loss. **Control over details**ensures that children and dependents are cared for and protected according to your wishes—guidance that continues even after you're gone. Each of these advantages helps families safeguard what matters most—not only in terms of money, but in peace of mind. Together, they make a **living trust** a powerful tool for shaping your legacy on your own terms.

Despite these strengths, misunderstandings about living trusts are common. Some people assume they're complicated to create or useful only for the wealthy. In truth, with a little guidance and a clear grasp of the key benefits, most families can establish a trust that fits their needs and removes much of the confusion surrounding estate planning.

Addressing Common Misconceptions and Fears

The privacy, flexibility, and probate-skipping features of living trusts catch the attention of adults wanting to protect their assets or streamline matters for their families. But almost as soon as people hear about the upsides, a mix of caution and skepticism often sets in. The old saying "too good to be true" echoes in many minds, especially with something as serious as legal planning. Misconceptions and fears leave a real mark on decisions here, holding people back from making choices that could help them.

Living Trusts Are Only For The Wealthy

A top myth claims that living trusts are just for millionaires or people with sprawling portfolios. Many middle-income earners or homeowners hear that only the ultra-rich use trusts and assume it's not the right tool for them. The reality is that living trusts offer strong benefits to those who want privacy, want to avoid probate, and want to organize their affairs cleanly, no matter their overall wealth. For example, a married couple with a modest home worried their assets were too small for a trust. Their attorney demonstrated to them how costly probate proceedings could ensnare even a single-family home if left solely to a will. With a living trust, their property could pass privately and easily to their children, skipping court delays.

Anyone who owns property, has accounts with beneficiary designations, or wants to make things easier for their loved ones can use a living trust. It's not about net worth; it's about control and giving clear instructions that reduce headaches for families.

Living Trusts Are Complicated and Expensive

Complexity, or the fear of unintentionally making a mistake, halts many individuals. They picture piles of paperwork, high lawyer fees, and a process reserved for legal experts. Some estate planning advertisements even stoke this fear, making the trust process sound like a secret code the average person can't crack. The truth is that living trusts, when "revocable" (changeable during your lifetime), don't add unnecessary layers for most people. They are meant to be adjusted as life changes. The real hurdle isn't complexity, but occasionally the lack of the right guidance.

Take the case of a single homeowner worried about paying thousands in legal costs. After talking to a fee-only estate planning attorney, she learned that setting up a basic revocable living trust can often cost about the same as a typical will plus advanced directives—only with fewer costs down the line for probate. Many states now allow guidance for filling out "pour-over" wills (which work with your trust) in simple, accessible ways. Ongoing fees are often minor. Some online horror stories make costs seem higher, but they often involve very complicated family or tax situations.

Living Trusts Mean Giving Up Control Over Assets

Hesitation often appears when the topic turns to **control**. Many people imagine that placing their bank accounts or homes into a trust means surrendering ownership or needing permission for every change. This confusion usually stems from mixing up **revocable** and **irrevocable** trusts. A **revocable living trust** allows its creator—known as the **grantor**—to change or dissolve the trust at any time, as long as they are alive and mentally capable. Owning assets "in trust" does not mean giving up control. If you name yourself as **trustee**, you can continue managing and spending those assets just as you always have.

One man in his early fifties recalled how a neighbor warned him he'd "never be able to sell" his truck once it was in a trust. Concerned, he checked with his estate adviser, who clarified that as trustee, he retained full authority to buy, sell, trade, or gift anything within the trust while he was alive. The paperwork might show the trust's name on the title, but the decision-making power remained entirely his. Unless a trust is specifically designed to limit access—a rare choice for living trusts—the creator stays firmly in control.

Living Trusts Replace the Need for a Will—Or Other Myths About Effectiveness

Some sources blur the relationship between wills and trusts, making people think one cancels the other. In fact, both tools can work together. A living trust organizes the main assets you transfer into it. Anything you own that's not titled in the trust may still pass under your will. That's why many people have a simple "pour-over" will to catch anything left outside the trust and move it over at death.

Confusion also arises when people see headlines about trust disputes. These stories often involve problems outside the trust itself: poor updates, inadequate communication, or deliberate fraud. Careful record-keeping and periodic review minimize these issues. Reliable information often comes from state bar associations, certified planning attorneys, or the official court resources. Relying on viral online stories or unverified social media posts can lead to stress or missteps.

Spotting Reliable Guidance and Moving Forward

Checking credentials and looking for plain, clear language in legal explanations helps filter out noise. Official state or national bar groups' resources, books by neutral professionals, and direct communication with known lawyers or planners beat rumor every time. Feeling empowered starts with knowing where myths come from, how living trusts really work, and how to match your plan to your needs. With time spent on solid information, you can plan with added confidence and less confusion, ready to use tools that fit your life, not someone else's story.

Bringing It All Together

Now that you understand the basics of living trusts—their purpose, key terms, and how they differ from wills—you are better equipped to make informed decisions that protect your assets and ease the burden on your loved ones. By choosing a living trust, you can ensure privacy, avoid lengthy probate delays, and maintain control over how and when your property is shared. With clear knowledge removing common fears and misconceptions, you can confidently explore the next steps in estate planning, creating a plan that fits your unique needs and offers peace of mind for you and your family's future.

CHAPTER 14

IS A LIVING TRUST RIGHT FOR YOU?

Have you ever wondered how to protect your family's future without leaving them caught in long, expensive court battles? What if your property is spread across multiple states, or you own a small business that needs steady management when you're no longer able to lead it? Many people wrestle with these questions quietly, unsure which tools truly fit their situation. Some worry that the legal documents will be too complicated; others hesitate to plan at all, uncertain whether their wishes will be honored exactly as they intend.

These concerns are both common and deeply human. They encapsulate the essence of estate planning—ensuring the well-being of those you cherish after your passing. This chapter invites you to explore whether a **living trust** might be the right solution for your needs, helping you understand how it compares to other options and whether it offers the control, privacy, and peace of mind you're looking for.

Who Benefits from a Living Trust: Typical and Special Circumstances

Deciding who benefits most from a living trust begins with looking at property owners. Homeowners and anyone with real estate often face long, expensive probate if they only have a will. A living trust removes real property from probate, letting it pass directly to heirs. For instance, if a couple owns a home together, placing the property in a living trust lets the surviving partner or children take ownership with little delay or court cost. This direct route becomes even more valuable when someone holds property in multiple states, since each location typically requires its own probate case. With a living trust, these assets are managed under a single plan, saving time and legal fees.

Owning other assets, such as investment accounts, family businesses, or second homes, can also motivate people to set up a living trust. Someone running a small business, for example, risks interruption for employees and clients if they die without clear instructions for who takes over. By naming a successor trustee in the trust, a business owner ensures continued management or simple closure. This could mean naming an adult child to run the shop, dividing business shares among siblings, or selling the business and splitting profits. No matter the plan, the living trust keeps decisions private and immediate, out of the probate court.

For parents and grandparents—especially those raising minor children or caring for dependents with disabilities—a **living trust** offers far greater control than a will. Consider a single parent with two children under 18. If they leave only a will, the court will manage any inheritance for the minors under strict rules with limited investment flexibility. When the children turn 18, they receive the full amount at once, even if the parent wanted the funds to support them gradually through college or other milestones. A living trust allows the parent to schedule distributions over time, fund education and healthcare, and appoint a trusted person to manage assets until the children are ready. For families with a child who has special needs, a trust can also prevent direct inheritance that might jeopardize eligibility for government assistance—while ensuring lifelong financial support.

Blended families and those experiencing remarriage often benefit from the extra clarity and protection a trust provides. Imagine someone with children from a first marriage and a current spouse. Depending solely on a will could lead to conflict over who inherits the family home or personal belongings. A living trust can separate inheritances clearly—for example, granting the current spouse use of the home for life while reserving ownership for the children later. This structure helps prevent disputes and reduces the likelihood of costly court battles.

People planning for **declining health**—their own or a loved one's—also gain from the flexibility of a living trust. If the trust creator becomes ill or incapacitated, a named **successor trustee** can immediately take over financial management without court involvement. Bills continue to be paid, investments maintained, and dependents cared for, eliminating the need for guardianship or conservatorship proceedings. For retirees, this layer of assurance becomes especially valuable.

Finally, **privacy** is one of the strongest reasons people choose a living trust. Wills must pass through probate, becoming part of the public record—meaning banks, neighbors, or even distant relatives can see your assets and who receives them. A living trust, by contrast, remains private. Only trustees and beneficiaries know its details, protecting both family privacy and heirs from unwanted attention or pressure.

Living trusts also help people with assets in more than one state by solving the challenge of multiple probate courts. A retiree owning vacation property in another state can include it in the trust, so heirs avoid having to hire lawyers in both locations. The trust centralizes all property, making the process seamless and coordinated.

Sometimes, family members need protection from their own circumstances. A parent may want to protect an adult child's inheritance from creditors, divorce settlements, or unwise spending. With a living trust, the trustee can hold funds until the child reaches a certain age or meets other conditions, protecting assets that a simple will might leave vulnerable.

Still, living trusts are not a catch-all. Some people with very simple assets or without concerns about minors or real estate may find a will that covers their needs. Wills remain vital for choosing guardians for minor children, naming funeral wishes, or passing on certain sentimental items. Legal experts often recommend integrating both tools—a living trust to avoid probate and manage assets, and a will to handle any property not included in the trust and to name guardians for young children. Each person's situation shapes the right estate plan, and using both gives flexible options and peace of mind for families with evolving needs.

The Continuing Role of Wills in Estate Planning

Advantages of a living trust often stand out: privacy, probate avoidance, and greater control over asset distribution. Yet property owners can overlook that a trust, even one tailored to their needs, cannot fully replace a will. A will serves as a critical safety net for family members, personal wishes, and unaddressed issues in the estate plan.

A will is a legal document that spells out a person's wishes for their property and responsibilities after death. Unlike a living trust, which can transfer ownership of certain assets to named beneficiaries while the grantor is still alive, a will becomes effective only at death and covers a larger set of personal matters. A trust mainly deals with assets held within it, but a will has a wider reach, directing the distribution of property not titled or transferred to the trust and handling family and personal concerns a trust just cannot.

Unique Functions Served by a Will

Some roles are unique to a will. One of the most vital is the appointment of a guardian for minor children. A trust cannot make guardianship designations; only a will lets parents choose who will raise their children if both are gone. Without this direction, state courts will decide, which may not match a parent's wishes.

A will also deals with personal property not formally assigned to the trust. This might mean favorite pieces of jewelry, family heirlooms, cars, artwork, or even sentimental gifts promised but not documented elsewhere. If a person acquires new property and forgets to retitle it into the trust, the will captures those items and clarifies where they go.

Real-World Scenarios Where a Will Remains Indispensable

- **Guardianship Needs**: A single parent with a living trust still needs a will to state who will care for children in their absence. If no will exists, guardianship decisions fall to the courts, often based on family hierarchy or local law rather than personal preference.
- **Unfunded Property**: Imagine a homeowner who refinances and retitles the house back into personal ownership but passes away before transferring it back into the trust. The house falls outside the trust—only a will can direct its distribution.
- **Personal Gifts**: Someone collects rare stamps and stores them in a safe deposit box. They never move the collection into the trust. The will details who inherits the stamps, making sure this personal wish is honored.
- **Recently Acquired Assets**: If an individual receives a car inheritance close to death, there may not be time to transfer it into the trust. The will steps in as the safety net for such assets.

The Role and Importance of a Pour-Over Will

The pour-over will is a practical solution for those who have a living trust. This special type of will acts like a catch-all, stating that any items or property not placed into the trust during life should be transferred ("poured over") into the trust at death. Assets outside the trust still go through probate, but they ultimately end up managed as intended within the trust's framework. A pour-over will is vital because no matter how careful someone is, there is often something left out.

Action Steps for Integrating a Will and Living Trust

Reviewing all assets is crucial. Start by listing everything owned—real estate, vehicles, investment accounts, personal items. Check each item's title and beneficiary designation. For each asset, decide: should it go into the trust, pass through a beneficiary form, or remain outside and be covered by the will? Retitle real estate, financial accounts, and other major assets into the trust as needed. Double-check that new assets are handled in a timely manner.

Keep both documents—the will and the trust—up to date. Major life changes like births, deaths, marriages, and divorces call for immediate review. Update guardianship choices for children, add new property to the trust, and modify bequests for personal items in the will as relationships and circumstances evolve.

Consulting with an estate planning professional can prevent costly mistakes, such as overlapping or conflicting terms between documents. Many assume a living trust automatically replaces the need for a will, but this is not true. A will remains necessary for everything that trust cannot reach.

Maximizing the Power of Both Tools

A trust directs major assets; a will gives instructions for remaining wishes and property. Both work together to cover gaps and avoid mistakes. Careful coordination of asset titles, beneficiary forms, and document terms ensures smooth handling of property and personal matters. Regular review of assets, attention to personal wishes, and professional guidance when needed combine to create a working, flexible plan.

As people's lives change, the living trust's flexibility and revocable nature can adapt to new family or property needs. This means readers can remain confident that their estate plan will continue to serve their goals, and they will be ready to learn more about how revocable living trusts keep pace with life's changes.

Flexibility of Revocable Living Trusts

Wills usually outline what happens after you die, but they don't always allow for quick or easy adjustments while you're alive. Life keeps moving—families grow, priorities shift, and circumstances change—and that's where the flexibility of a **revocable living trust** truly stands out. A revocable living trust is a legal arrangement in which you, as the trust maker (or **grantor**), place your assets—homes, savings, investments, or even a small business—into a trust that you control completely as long as you remain mentally capable. You decide who receives what, when, and under what conditions, while keeping the power to revise your plan whenever life takes a new direction.

A revocable living trust grows and adapts with you. If your family changes—a new grandchild is born, a child marries, loved ones relocate, or relationships evolve—the trust adjusts easily. You might sell a house, start a business, or acquire new investments over the years. At these pivotal moments, the trust does not confine you or compel you to begin anew. Instead, you can add or remove beneficiaries, update asset lists, or even change your successor trustee with minimal effort.

There are two main ways to update your trust: **amendments** and **restatements.** An **amendment** works like an update to a contract—you create a short document specifying what you want to change, sign it, and attach it to your existing trust. It's ideal for smaller updates, such as adding a new beneficiary after a marriage or birth. For example, if your daughter welcomes a baby, you can simply amend the trust to include your new grandchild as a beneficiary. Or, if you decide to give a family heirloom to someone different, a quick amendment updates your wishes instantly.

A **restatement** is broader in scope. When you want to make multiple changes or reorganize your trust's language, you can restate the entire document while keeping the same name and date. This avoids confusion later and keeps titles and account ownership intact. You (and your co-trustee, if applicable) sign the restatement and store it with your existing paperwork. For major life changes—such as relocating to a new state, selling significant property, or restructuring your estate after a divorce—a restatement provides a fresh start without having to dissolve the old trust or re-title every asset.

People often worry that these updates require long meetings or big lawyer bills. In reality, as long as you're mentally capable, changes are usually straightforward—sometimes even a single page. Many families handle simple amendments themselves using templates, or they pay for a single session with a professional. If your trust gets complex or holds lots of property, an estate planner can guide you, but the process remains much easier and more private than redoing a will or creating an irrevocable trust.

Picture a family-owned business that expands after a decade. The parents want to include their two adult children and a son-in-law as beneficiaries while putting guidelines on selling shares. With a revocable trust, they amend the document to add the new family members and set the instructions without re-signing all the business property. Or, think about a blended family, newly married with stepchildren on both sides. Updating the trust means including everyone important, adjusting amounts left to each person, and making sure parent and stepparent wishes are honored. There's no need to start over from scratch or risk missing someone.

Homeowners sometimes choose to downsize in retirement, selling a long-time house and moving closer to family. The new property and any profits slide directly into the trust by updating the asset listing—no need to make a new will or start a new trust. The same goes for adding new bank accounts or selling off investments; the changes are managed by updating your trust schedule and, when needed, a simple amendment.

Flexibility also means full control over the assets in the trust. The trust maker can invest, buy or sell property, add or remove beneficiaries, attach new conditions, and even revoke (officially cancel) the trust at any time. Nothing is locked until death or incapacity, providing strong reassurance that your wishes stay current with your life. If your best friend, chosen as a future trustee, moves abroad and can't help, you swap in someone local with an amendment.

Comparing estate planning options makes this clear:

- **Revocable living trust:** Can be changed or cancelled by maker at any time while alive and capable; assets added or removed easily; beneficiaries updated as life shifts.
- **Wills:** Must be revised or replaced each time you want changes. Final and public at death, more formal.
- **Irrevocable trusts:** Cannot be adapted after setup except in rare cases—no way to change beneficiaries or reclaim assets.

Flexibility enables you to respond to joys, setbacks, and surprises with confidence. Your plan keeps pace with your family, assets, and wishes. This makes a revocable living trust a strong comfort for anyone hoping estate planning will serve not only today's needs but the ones still to come.

Bringing It All Together

Now that you understand how a living trust can protect your assets, provide for loved ones, and adapt to life's changes, you are better equipped to decide if it fits your unique estate planning needs. By carefully considering who benefits, acknowledging the ongoing importance of a will, and embracing the flexibility of revocable trusts, you can create a comprehensive plan that avoids probate, safeguards privacy, and offers peace of mind. As your family grows and circumstances evolve, this knowledge empowers you to take practical steps—whether updating documents or seeking professional advice—so your estate plan remains strong, clear, and tailored to secure your legacy well into the future.

CHAPTER 15
PLANNING YOUR TRUST—WHAT TO DECIDE BEFORE YOU WRITE IT

Have you ever paused to consider what truly needs to be decided before creating a trust? How do you ensure every important detail is covered so your wishes are clear and your loved ones are protected? Many people begin drafting a trust without fully understanding the key choices involved, which can lead to confusion, delays, or unintended consequences. Before putting pen to paper, essential decisions about what property to include, who will manage it, who benefits from it, and how distributions should work must be thoughtfully made. This chapter will guide you through those crucial considerations, helping you build a solid foundation for your trust planning that avoids common pitfalls and sets the stage for a smooth transfer of your assets.

Assessing and Listing Your Assets for the Trust

Building a trust begins with a clear, detailed list of everything a person owns that might fit within a trust. Recognizing the necessity of this list can make what looks overwhelming feel manageable. Assets, in this context, are anything of value you have legal claim to —property, money, shares, retirement funds, business interests, personal valuables, and even digital assets like intellectual property and royalties. For trust planning, assets can be grouped into two categories: probate and non-probate property. Probate property includes assets that would, without a trust, pass through a court-supervised estate process after death—things owned solely in your name with no specific beneficiary. Non-probate property passes directly to another person or entity upon your death, such as accounts or insurance policies with named beneficiaries, or property held jointly with right of survivorship.

Both asset types deserve careful review, as trusts often cover both, though the method may differ. Real estate is usually the most valuable asset for many. This covers not only a person's primary residence but also vacation homes, rental properties, or land. Cash and bank accounts—checking, savings, and certificates of deposit—are straightforward. Investments and retirement accounts are vital but sometimes tricky. Standard brokerage accounts can often be retitled in the name of a trust, but tax-advantaged retirement accounts like IRAs or 401(k)s usually cannot have ownership transferred while the original owner is alive. Life insurance policies can list a trust as beneficiary, allowing proceeds to pass to the trust, though policies themselves typically do not transfer.

Other investment assets, like stocks, bonds, mutual funds, annuities, and health savings accounts, should also be considered. Business ownership adds another layer. Sole proprietorships, shares in a family company, or interests in partnerships or LLCs might be placed into a trust, but partnership or corporate agreements sometimes limit transfers; it's wise to review legal documents before listing these.

Personal property, such as vehicles, boats, and even airplanes, might also be included, depending on value and state law. Significant personal items often carry more meaning than monetary worth: jewelry, collections, art, antiques, or family heirlooms can go into a trust for clear transfer and to avoid disputes. Intellectual property—copyrights, patents, trademarks, and royalties—should be inventoried and may be placed in a trust, so long as ownership is clear.

Here's an example of a diverse asset inventory:

- Primary residence (123 Oak Lane)
- Vacation home (Lakeview Cabin)
- Checking account at Neighborhood Bank
- Brokerage account with mutual funds and bonds
- IRA (cannot transfer ownership to trust, but can list trust as beneficiary)
- Shares in Johnson Family LLC
- 2019 Toyota Camry
- Valuable watch collection
- Life insurance policy (XYZ Life Insurers)
- Copyrights from published books
- Art and rare coin collections

Identifying these assets is only the beginning. A practical method involves moving step-by-step. First, walk room by room in each property, making a list of all real estate owned, then noting valuable personal items found in each space. This includes garages, safety deposit boxes, attics, and storage units. Next, gather financial documents: bank account statements, investment summaries, retirement plan details, insurance policies, business documents, deeds, and titles. Review digital records as well, like online payment accounts or cryptocurrency holdings.

Gather documents that prove ownership—titles, deeds, share certificates, beneficiary statements, contracts, and appraisals. Write the current estimated value beside each item on your list. You don't need formal appraisals unless values are unclear; a reasonable market estimate is sufficient for planning. Because life changes—marriage, divorce, the birth of a child, or acquiring or selling assets—update this list during major milestones so it remains accurate and reliable.

Some assets involve **joint ownership** or **named beneficiaries.** For example, property owned with a spouse or business partner may pass automatically outside of probate, unless the co-owner has already passed away. Accounts with "transfer on death" (TOD) or "payable on death" (POD) designations, as well as insurance policies or retirement plans listing specific beneficiaries, may not need to be included in a trust unless you want different instructions or additional control. In these cases, confirm directly with each financial institution how those accounts will transfer.

When ownership details are uncertain—or when describing a business interest—it's wise to consult a lawyer or tax professional. However, compiling your list and gathering documentation can happen first. Once your asset inventory is complete, later steps in trust planning become far simpler. The next step—**choosing your trustee and backup**—naturally follows once you have a clear picture of your estate. In the next section, we'll explore how to select the people or institutions best equipped to carry out your wishes with care and precision.

Appointing Trustees and Identifying Beneficiaries

Choosing who will manage your trust is the next clear step after you have listed your assets. Your chosen trustee will oversee the meticulous execution of your instructions. A trustee's job reaches beyond simply handing out property—this is someone who must handle money, pay bills, settle debts, file tax forms, and keep records that might later be needed by both the trust's beneficiaries and outside organizations like the IRS. Organization and reliability matter a lot. If someone is regularly late with their own bills or sometimes lets details slip, overseeing a trust might not fit them. It also helps if the person stays clear of family arguments and can let go of their own opinions and follow written instructions.

What Makes a Strong Trustee

You can pick a family member, a close friend, or a professional such as a trust company, accountant, or lawyer. Many people think of their oldest child, but this approach does not fit all families. Ask yourself questions: Does this person handle stress well? Can they be fair if children or siblings disagree? If you sense rivalry or any history of putting one person's needs above another, think twice. Also consider work and life circumstances—does your possible trustee have time to do the job well?

Sometimes, naming a friend or someone outside your immediate family works better. A neutral party can keep things straightforward when emotions run high. For bigger trusts, or when property is spread between states, a professional trustee may help avoid costly mistakes. Professional trustees charge fees, but reliability is their business. But friends or family may know your needs better than a pro, and they might do it for free.

Real-World Example

Suppose Jim picks his eldest daughter, Sandra, because she is the oldest and lives nearby. Sandra tries, but paperwork piles up, and when her brother asks about the trust, she leaves his requests unanswered. Disagreements get worse. In another family, Alice chooses her sister-in-law, who acts calmly and lets everyone see the records. The process finishes without drama, and all instructions get carried out. Picking a trustee who is steady and clear-headed helps protect against both mistakes and hurt feelings.

Why You Need a Successor Trustee

Even the best trustee can become unwilling or unable to serve because of illness, work, or death. A successor trustee steps in if the first trustee can't continue. Without a backup, your trust might need a court to appoint someone, which can take time and open old wounds. Clearly listing a successor helps everything stay on track and keeps your wishes at the center of every step.

Picking Your Beneficiaries—and Their Backups

A primary beneficiary is your first choice—this is the person or charity meant to receive your assets. A backup (sometimes called "contingent beneficiary") will inherit only if the primary beneficiary can't, because of death or any other reason.

Steps for Naming Beneficiaries

1. Write down can't because a group you want to inherit, using full names.
2. Choose whether to name people individually or by group, such as "my children, in equal shares."
3. If you name a child who is a minor, think about naming a guardian to manage their share.
4. For blended families, be clear—if you mean biological children only or want stepchildren included, write that down.
5. For charities or organizations, use their full legal names to avoid confusion.

Scenario: You name your sister as the primary beneficiary, but if she passes away before you, you want her daughter to inherit. You can write, "to my sister, Jane Smith," or, if she is not living, "to her daughter, Emily Smith." This step makes sure the property doesn't go somewhere you never intended.

Managing Complicated Family Situations

Families change over the years. Divorces, remarriages, estrangement, or new grandchildren call for careful thinking. In these cases, spelling out exactly who gets what helps avoid hurt and legal fights. For blended or uncertain relationships, some write, "to my spouse and all children born to or legally adopted by me, in equal shares." If you want to exclude someone, it should be direct and unmistakable within the trust. If you want an estranged child to inherit, but only under certain conditions, a clear description helps.

Reviewing your beneficiary choices regularly is wise, especially after big changes like marriage, divorce, or birth of a grandchild. Your trust remains effective only if your choices match your real wishes as life carries on.

Smooth trustee appointments and carefully listed beneficiaries lay the groundwork for organized asset transfer. Who you name and how you define their shares mean your values will shape what happens to everything you leave behind. Deciding how, when, and under what terms those assets get divided comes next.

Determining Asset Distribution Plans

Deciding how and when to distribute assets is about making your intentions clear for the people you trust. The roles you assign—whether a thoughtful individual as your trustee or diligent alternates to step in if needed—affect the path your trust will follow and the lives of your beneficiaries. Each choice about who receives assets and when can influence how your family interacts for years to come.

Common ways to distribute trust assets

Several approaches stand out when deciding how assets should reach your beneficiaries. Outright distribution gives them everything at once, usually after your death or another fixed event. This way works well for mature adults with responsible spending habits or for relatively small estates where further oversight seems unnecessary. It offers speed and simplicity. Nevertheless, giving a large sum to a young or inexperienced heir can bring risks of poor decisions, temptation for creditors, or challenges during divorce settlements.

Staggered distributions divide the payout into pieces delivered over time or at set milestones. For instance:

- One-third at age 25
- Half the remainder at 30
- Balance at 35

This method can encourage long-term financial maturity, since beneficiaries have time to learn from earlier experiences. It also comforts parents or grandparents who worry about reckless spending with a sudden windfall. Drawbacks include added administrative work for your trustee and possible frustrations for beneficiaries who want or need more flexibility.

Conditional distributions tie payouts to specific achievements or life events. Some conditions people use include:

- Graduation from college
- Marriage
- Maintaining employment
- Completing addiction treatment

A trust might say, "Distribute up to $20,000 upon proof of a bachelor's degree," or "Release funds for the down payment of a first home." These conditions can motivate your beneficiaries, but they work best when requirements are simple to prove. Overly complex or vague wishes can leave your trustee stuck in the middle if someone disagrees about whether a condition was met.

Pros and cons at a glance

- **Outright:** Quick, no red tape, but risk of careless spending
- **Staggered: It promotes responsibility and safeguards youth, but requires longer oversight.**
- **Conditional:** Encourages goals and personal growth, but can frustrate or delay access

Considering timing and its impact

The moment a beneficiary receives their share shapes what they do with it. Immediate access brings instant freedom, yet some people prefer to delay distributions. They do this to help protect minors or shield assets from creditors, lawsuits, or even divorce settlements. A trust can set twenty-one, twenty-five, or thirty as the magic ages for large gifts, reducing a spendthrift risk.

Some families use the trust to pay only for educational or medical costs while someone is a minor, then open the rest of the funds after age thirty. Grandparents may wish to see grandchildren's college costs covered and then have any unspent funds released as young adults reach financial independence.

Delays can cause tension if someone feels entitled to "their" money, so clear communication within the trust is helpful. Some people include a note explaining choices, like "I want each heir to fully complete college before receiving the entire gift," so wishes feel rooted in care, not control.

Writing clear, precise instructions

Trustees need directions that leave no room for guessing. Saying "divide equally between my children" works better than "as you see fit," which risks confusion and arguments. Phrasing like "pay each grandchild $10,000 for tuition to an accredited college" makes intentions direct and avoids gaps.

Families with children from more than one marriage may need extra clarity: "After selling the home, give fifty percent of the proceeds to my daughter, Jane, and twenty-five percent each to my sons, Rick and Thomas." Anticipate what questions might come up, such as, "Does someone qualify as a beneficiary if adopted after your death?" If a child dies first, can their share be passed on to their own children? A little extra detail in your writing lets trustees act with confidence and prevents misunderstandings.

Balancing control with flexibility

Desiring order shouldn't block smart decisions in emergencies. A trust can let your trustee use skills and judgment you trusted them for in the first place. You might write, "You may make early distributions for severe medical needs or approved emergencies as you deem prudent." By drawing clear boundaries—like capping extra payouts or limiting them to family, not creditors—you give both direction and breathing room.

Some families limit trustee discretion to prevent favoritism, while others want their trustee to help beneficiaries with unforeseen crises. Outlining these wishes gives your trustee confidence to act and keeps everything fair. Simple steps, real examples, and your personal touch combine to create strong instructions that reflect what you value most.

Bringing It All Together

Thoughtful planning of your assets, trustees, beneficiaries, and distribution methods forms the foundation of a successful trust that honors your wishes and protects your family's future. By carefully assessing what you own and choosing reliable people to manage and receive those assets, you can prevent confusion, delays, and disputes later on. Clear instructions about how and when assets will be shared give your trustee the confidence to act wisely while providing your beneficiaries with security and fairness. Now that you have a solid inventory and understand the key decisions ahead, you are ready to move forward with drafting your trust, turning your plans into a clear, actionable document that brings lasting peace of mind.

CHAPTER 16
CREATING THE TRUST—STEP-BY-STEP WITHOUT A LAWYER

"I just don't know where to start," Maria whispered, staring at the blank screen before her. The forms, the legal words, the instructions—it all felt like a tangled mess that could easily lead to mistakes. She wanted to create a trust for her children, something clear and solid, but without paying sky-high lawyer fees. Meanwhile, across town, Steve scanned a free template he had found online. It seemed simple enough, but as he filled in the blanks, questions about his blended family's needs nagged at him. Was this really enough to protect everything? Could he get it done on his own without missing something important?

These moments are familiar for many who decide to take control of their estate plans without an attorney. The path isn't always obvious, and the choices about how to draft your trust can feel overwhelming. Finding the right approach means balancing ease, cost, and confidence while avoiding common errors that could undo months or years of effort. Yet with clear steps and practical tools, setting up a trust independently is not only possible—it can offer peace of mind knowing your wishes are written down and ready to stand up in court if needed.

Behind the hesitation and uncertainty lies a straightforward process broken into manageable parts. Each decision—from selecting your drafting method to signing the final document—shapes how well your trust will serve you and those you care about. This chapter guides you through those decisions and provides the roadmap to navigate the complexities calmly, helping you build a legally sound trust without needing a lawyer at every turn.

Choosing Your Drafting Method and Avoiding Common Pitfalls

Understanding how to start creating a trust without an attorney means choosing a method that lines up with your confidence, your family's needs, and your level of comfort filling out legal documents. You have three proven ways to draft your trust on your own: DIY software, packaged trust kits, and downloadable templates. Each offers a different mix of support, cost, and flexibility.

DIY trust software offers a guided, step-by-step experience on your computer or tablet. These programs function like wizards: they ask about your family, property, and wishes, then generate a trust by filling in the necessary legal language. If you encounter a difficult question, many include help menus or chat support. Most also stay updated with current state laws and automatically check for missing information or common errors before you print and sign. You typically pay a one-time fee of about **$60–$120**. This approach works best for those who want guided support, have straightforward family needs (such as leaving everything evenly to children or a spouse), and want extra assurance that state requirements are met. The main drawback comes with complex situations—blended families, special needs dependents, or unusual assets—where the software may lack flexibility or limit custom instructions.

Printed or digital trust kits provide another user-friendly path. These include explanations, glossaries, and step-by-step checklists for completing the documents yourself. The trust form is either pre-printed or downloadable, and you fill in the blanks by hand or using a word processor. Kits generally cost **$25–$60** and are easy to find online or in major bookstores. They suit people who prefer a tangible guide and like seeing everything laid out on paper. The included examples help beginners get started confidently. However, kits rarely include ongoing updates, meaning their advice may not reflect recent state law changes. Their checklists also catch only basic mistakes, offering less protection against contradictions or state-specific signature rules.

Downloadable or fill-in-the-blank templates are the quickest and least expensive option. These are simple Word or PDF files with blank fields for your information. Some are free, while premium versions run about **$10–$30**. Templates offer total flexibility for those who already understand trust basics and want to customize every detail. However, because they lack glossaries or built-in guidance, there's a higher risk of missing key requirements or including wording that doesn't align with your state's laws. Templates work best for experienced DIYers—often those with legal or estate-planning knowledge—who are confident reviewing their own work.

Choosing the Right Fit: Two Example Scenarios

Maria is a single parent who owns a small home and wants everything to go equally to her two children. She feels nervous about missing a step, so she buys DIY trust software. The guided questions keep her on track, and the program double-checks her state's signature rules. The process feels safe, and Maria gets a printout ready for her to sign and notarize.

In contrast, Steve wants a trust for his blended family. He downloads a free template to save money. It doesn't cover stepchildren, and he forgets to include key property. Months later, he finds out that courts may not honor his wishes because the template language didn't match his family situation or property list. Steve's mistake shows that saving money upfront can cost you in clarity and enforceability.

Common Mistakes to Avoid

- Using generic language from a template that doesn't match your family or property

  Not changing sections or leaving standard phrases can mean the courts have trouble understanding or following your wishes. Always update template text to reflect your own details. Read each section aloud to check if it really fits your plan.

- Forgetting state signature requirements

  Some states need witnesses and notarization on the main trust or the property schedules. Missing these can mean your trust is not valid. To avoid this, check your state's rules and have all needed signatures and notarizations before storing the document.

- Not transferring property into the trust

  Many people write their trust but forget to legally move their property titles, accounts, or deeds into the trust's name. If you don't, the trust remains empty. Gather a list of assets, use your trust's legal name, and follow up by changing deeds, titles, or account registrations as your bank or state requires.

Strong, clear instructions and a direct drafting method make the path to a successful trust easiest to follow. Taking control with the approach that fits your needs lays the groundwork for building a document that will protect your assets and honor your wishes in every detail. Trust creation works best when you have the right tools and a clear understanding of each step ahead.

Composing the Trust Document: Sample Language and Walkthrough

Choosing your drafting method—software, template, or kit—sets the stage for creating your trust document. After reviewing your options and picking the method that fits your comfort level, you can shift confidently into drafting. Your role now is to capture your wishes clearly, step by step, on paper. Each part of the document matters and deserves careful attention.

Trust Title and Introductory Clause

Start with a clear, simple title at the top, like "John Doe Revocable Living Trust." This lets anyone review your paperwork and immediately know what it is. Below the title, write an introductory sentence to establish the purpose and the trust's date. Use plain language such as

"This Trust Agreement is made on June 1, 2024, by John Doe of 123 Elm Street, City, State."

The introductory clause sets the foundation. It lists the trust creator (called the grantor or settlor), the original trustee, and the date the trust goes into effect. This opening creates a record and draws a line marking your assets as trust property from this point forward.

Declaration of Trust

A basic declaration states that you are transferring your property into the trust and naming yourself—often the grantor—as the initial trustee. Here's how to make this direct:

"I, John Doe, declare that I am creating this revocable living trust and serving as its initial trustee. I transfer ownership of the assets listed in this document to this trust."

If you want your spouse to serve as co-trustee, just name both of you: "John Doe and Jane Doe, as co-trustees."

Trustee and Successor Trustee Provisions

This part identifies who will carry out your wishes and manage the trust property now and after you cannot. Start by naming yourself or the primary trustee:

"The initial trustee shall be John Doe."

Then name at least one successor trustee, the person or people you trust to step in if needed. Add their contact information to avoid any confusion. Example:

"If I am unable or unwilling to serve as trustee, I nominate Jane Doe, 456 Maple Lane, City, State, as successor trustee."

Including successors makes sure the trust does not go in limbo if you become incapacitated or pass away. Spell out what counts as "unable" or "unwilling" if you wish—"unable" could mean medically unfit, for instance.

Property Schedule

A detailed list of each asset you want the trust to own keeps matters clear. In a section called "Schedule A" or similar, describe each asset. Group homes, accounts, and valuables separately. If you own real estate, describe each place in full:

- 123 Oak Street, City, State (Main Residence)
- 456 Pine Lane, City, State (Vacation Cabin)

For accounts or valuables, say:

- Savings account ending in 1234 at City Bank
- 2015 Honda CR-V, VIN: 1HGXXXXXXXXX
- Shares of ABC Corporation (50 shares), held at XYZ Brokerage

Be thorough—if you forget an asset, it might bypass the trust and go through probate. List each valuable item or property you want included, plain and simple.

Beneficiary Designations

List people or organizations who will receive assets. Use full names and relationships for individuals. For blended families, separate lines for each child or stepchild helps prevent disputes.

"Upon my death, I give all trust property in equal shares to my children: Emily Doe and Ryan Doe."

For charities:

"I give $10,000 to the Animal Shelter, EIN 12-3456789, located at 101 Pet Lane, City, State."

Ambiguity in beneficiary names leads to confusion or even legal battles, so write exactly who or what you mean.

Distribution Instructions

Clearly explain how you want your property divided. If you want a child to receive their share at a certain age, note it simply:

"Emily Doe will receive her share at age 25. Until then, the trustee may use the funds for her health and education at their discretion."

For unequal shares or special situations, spell out the percentages or conditions. Example for stepchildren:

"Ryan Doe receives 60%, and Lisa Smith (stepdaughter) receives 40%."

Review this part twice. If you write "children" but do not list names, a court might interpret your intent in a way you do not expect.

Final Thoughts on Drafting

Keep your language short, direct, and free from extra details. Courts and banks look for clarity—not fancy words or legal terms. Check each section for missing names, outdated addresses, or assets you may have overlooked. Avoid vague phrases like "as my family sees fit," which create uncertainty.

Once each part is in place, your document is almost ready to protect your wishes. Before it becomes official, you will need the right signatures, witnesses, and notarization. These last steps make the trust binding and recognized in law, ensuring your efforts carry full power for your loved ones.

Executing Your Trust: Witnessing and Notarizing Procedures

Holding a completed draft of your trust puts you in a strong position, but that document won't hold up in court—or at a bank—until it's properly executed. **Execution** means completing the legal steps that make your trust official, recognized, and protected against disputes. Skipping or mishandling even one step can lead to confusion, delays, or worse—your trust could be rejected, leaving your wishes and assets vulnerable. Banks, title companies, and courts honor only those trusts that meet strict legal standards. Following clear, predictable steps eliminates these risks and ensures your plan stands firm.

Each state sets its own **rules for witnesses**, but most require at least two. Witnesses serve as neutral observers who confirm you were of sound mind and acted voluntarily. The best witnesses are adults who are not mentioned anywhere in your trust. By law, beneficiaries—anyone set to inherit—cannot serve as witnesses. This prevents claims of undue influence or forged signatures. For example, if your daughter acts as a witness while also being a beneficiary, a court could later declare the trust invalid or require her to give up her share. Instead, choose witnesses such as a cousin, coworker, or friend who isn't named in the trust. Both must be present during the entire signing and willing to confirm your intent if ever questioned.

Here's how this plays out in real life: John creates a trust leaving everything to his friend Mike and asks Mike to serve as a witness. Years later, John's relatives challenge the trust in court. Because Mike signed as both witness and beneficiary, the judge invalidates the document—or at least removes Mike's inheritance. This simple mistake is entirely avoidable by choosing witnesses with no stake in the trust. Always double-check the document before anyone signs, and confirm that all witnesses are fully eligible.

Signing in the presence of witnesses follows a precise sequence. Use this standard procedure:

1. Gather everyone in the same room: you (the trust creator) and both witnesses.
2. Bring the unsigned, printed trust document and valid identification for yourself and your witnesses.
3. Verbally state your intention to sign the trust and have each witness do the same.
4. Sign your name in the designated spot as creator or "grantor."
5. Each witness, one after the other, signs below or beside your signature. They must see you sign, and you must see them sign. No one should leave the room until all signatures are complete.
6. If your state requires a notary at the same time, the notary should watch the entire process.

A signed trust gains even more strength once it's notarized. Notarization means an official "notary public" stamps your document after checking your identity. This proves the signatures are real and that you have not been pressured or impersonated. Notarization helps block fraud, and banks or courts often insist on it before they honor your instructions. Most adults can find a notary at their main bank branch, credit union, law office, UPS store, or through online notary platforms that offer video meetings for this purpose. Bring a government-issued ID, your unsigned trust, and your witnesses if your state or notary asks for them. Only sign in the notary's presence to ensure authenticity.

States share many basic rules, but a few add extra requirements such as more witnesses or using special paper. Before you sign, take five minutes to call your county clerk's office or visit your state's official court website. Ask if there are conditions for witnessing or notarizing a trust, such as a "self-proving affidavit" or extra signature pages. This short check prevents wasted effort and gives you peace of mind.

Keeping an eye out for common errors will keep your trust valid:

- Not having all parties present when signing
- Using a beneficiary or someone named in the trust as your witness
- Allowing witnesses to sign after you, or signing outside their presence
- Signing the trust before meeting the notary
- Failing to use a current, government-issued photo ID
- Missing a notary seal or incomplete notary section

Double-check the final document before you file it away. All required signatures, the notary's stamp, and dates must be clear and readable. Store the executed (officially signed and sealed) trust in a fireproof safe at home or a bank safe deposit box. Tell at least one family member or trusted friend where to find your trust if needed. An executed trust, correctly witnessed and notarized, is a legal shield—a clear set of directions that others must respect and follow.

Wrapping Up

Now that you understand the key methods and critical steps to create and execute a trust on your own, you are equipped to take control of your estate planning with confidence. By choosing the drafting approach that matches your needs and carefully following signature and notarization rules, you can build a clear, valid legal document that protects your assets and honors your wishes. With attention to detail and awareness of common pitfalls, your self-created trust will stand strong against challenges and avoid costly delays or confusion for your loved ones. This knowledge empowers you to move forward decisively, securing your family's financial future without relying on expensive legal help.

CHAPTER 17

FUNDING THE TRUST—MAKING IT LEGALLY EFFECTIVE

"Isn't signing the trust enough to protect everything?" a client once asked me after completing their estate plan. It's a common question, but one that often leads to serious problems if left unanswered. Creating a trust is an important first step in managing and passing on your assets, but it doesn't automatically control or protect what you own. Without properly funding the trust—making sure your property, accounts, and other valuables are legally transferred into it—the trust remains an empty shell.

This chapter explains why funding a trust is essential to make it effective, turning written instructions into real protection for your family and your legacy. You will learn the necessary actions to transfer ownership of various assets, from real estate to bank accounts and personal property, along with practical advice to avoid costly mistakes. By understanding these steps and following a clear, methodical process, you can ensure that your trust works as intended, sparing your loved ones unnecessary delays, expenses, and confusion.

Understanding What It Means to Fund a Trust and Why It's Essential

A trust, by itself, is just a document—a set of instructions written on paper and signed with the best intentions. Yet, this document does not actually do anything until it owns or controls property. "Funding" a trust means taking real steps to move ownership of your actual assets—like your house, savings, or investments—into the trust's name. This step turns the trust from words into a tool that can protect your wishes, avoid probate, and help your loved ones in the way you intend.

Many people believe their job is finished once they sign their revocable living trust, but the real work comes after. Unless you move your assets into the trust, it stays empty. Picture a safe: you can buy the world's most secure safe, set the perfect combination, and install it in your home, but if you never put anything inside, it cannot protect your valuables. A trust without assets works exactly the same way. You have crafted your safe, but you need to fill it for it to do its job.

Imagine a family where parents create a trust and appoint their two children as equal beneficiaries. They sign every form, pay for legal advice, and feel secure—yet they never change the title on their house, the ownership on their brokerage account, or the name on their savings account. When they pass away, these assets remain in their personal names. As a result, their accounts and property go through probate, a public and often slow court process, because the trust does not own anything. The court decides who receives the assets, and the process adds months or even years, along with costs and possible disputes among family members.

Now look at another family who creates a similar trust and follows through completely. The parents retitle their house and investment accounts to the trust. Their savings accounts and certificates of deposit are updated with the trust's name. They even check beneficiary designations for retirement accounts and life insurance, making sure they are consistent with their wishes. When these parents pass away, every asset "inside" the trust is not subject to probate. The trustee quickly and privately transfers everything to the children. There is no court drama, no public record, and no delay. The family avoids confusion and conflict. Their wishes are honored.

Assets that people often need to fund include real estate, bank accounts, investment accounts, stocks and bonds, and even valuable personal property. Each one requires a different process. For a house or condominium, this means signing and recording a new deed that lists the trust as the owner. For a checking or savings account, the bank changes the account title to the trust's name. Non-retirement investment accounts need the account name updated, while IRAs and life insurance might need you to change the beneficiary rather than transferring ownership outright.

Even smaller assets deserve attention. Jewelry, collectibles, or a family heirloom do not get titled formally. Instead, you list them on a written schedule or assignment to the trust. The key is that every type of asset needs its action—there is no automatic shortcut. Whenever you acquire new property—a new home, vehicle, or large bank deposit—consider how to bring it "under" your trust so it gets the same protection and passes directly to your loved ones.

Some skip or delay funding the trust because the process seems tedious. Yet, the true cost comes later: legal battles, lost privacy, and hard feelings among relatives all because the trust was never "filled" properly. Beneficiaries may face months of uncertainty, and your legacy can be put at risk. By funding your trust fully, you are thinking ahead for your family. You help them avoid court, skip paperwork headaches, save money, and keep details private.

A complete and well-funded trust gives you peace of mind. It eases stress and worry for your loved ones. It means that what you worked hard for gets where you want it to go, without strangers interfering or family members fighting. Now that you see why funding matters, you need to know exactly how to carry out these steps for each type of asset. The following guidance will walk you through the detailed process of making sure every item you own is protected by your trust.

Step-by-Step Guide: Transferring Property and Updating Ownership

A trust works only if the assets are actually placed under its control. Funding a trust means changing the legal ownership of property, accounts, and financial tools so that the trust, not any one individual, holds them. Without these clear transfers, a trust can be powerless, leaving assets outside and subject to delays or court procedures. Turning a signed trust into a real, working arrangement takes methodical steps, careful paperwork, and a close eye for details. Here's a guide to doing this for a range of common assets.

Transferring Real Estate into the Trust

Real estate rarely moves automatically into a trust; it must be retitled. This typically requires preparing a new deed that names the trustee as the property owner. A standard example: John and Mary Smith prepare a new deed for their house at 123 Oak Avenue that reads, "John and Mary Smith, Trustees of the Smith Family Trust dated 06/15/2023."

The steps are as follows:

1. Get a copy of the current deed and the property's legal description.
2. Prepare a new deed document, such as a quitclaim or warranty deed, listing the trust as the new owner.
3. Ensure the deed uses correct legal names and the full trust title and date.
4. Sign the deed before a notary.
5. Submit the signed deed to the local county recorder or land records office, where it's filed and made part of the public record.

Example Deed Language

This QUITCLAIM DEED, made this ___ day of _____, 20__, by John Smith and Mary Smith, husband and wife, granting to John Smith and Mary Smith, Trustees of the Smith Family Trust dated 06/15/2023, the property described as follows: [legal description here].

Some states require extra steps, such as filing transfer tax documents or notifying the lender, especially if there's a mortgage. Always use the correct deed form for your state.

Funding Bank Accounts and Investments

Bank accounts, CDs, and brokerage accounts are often still in an individual's name until retitled. Banks and brokerages each have policies for trust transfers. Normally, you'll need:

- A copy of the trust document's title page and signature pages
- A certificate or abstract of trust (summarizes trust details for the bank)
- Valid identification for trustees

Write to your bank using language like:

"Please retitle savings account ending in 1234 to 'John Smith, Trustee, Smith Family Trust dated 06/15/2023.' Enclosed are copies of the trust and required identification."

Some banks may also have a trust account application to complete. For investment accounts, the custodial institution will walk you through transferring ownership or opening a new trust-titled account, moving assets from the old registration.

Using TOD and POD Designations

For accounts where retitling is complicated, consider a Transfer on Death (TOD) or Payable on Death (POD) designation. This tells the bank to pay the funds to your trust directly after death, instead of into the estate. Use designations like

"TOD – Smith Family Trust, dated 06/15/2023."

Retirement accounts, such as IRAs or 401(k)s, often work best by updating the beneficiary designation, not by changing ownership.

Updating Beneficiary and Ownership Forms

For life insurance, annuities, or retirement plans, ask for a beneficiary change form from the company. The proper way to fill this out to benefit the trust might be

"Primary Beneficiary: John Smith and Mary Smith, Trustees of the Smith Family Trust dated 06/15/2023."

Confirm the spelling, punctuation, and dates exactly match your trust documents. If the beneficiary language is wrong—wrong trust name, missing date, incomplete titles—the payout could end up going through probate or to the wrong party.

Funding Other Types of Property

Personal property like vehicles, valuable collections, or business ownership interests also needs attention. High-value items such as cars may require a new title application with the department of motor vehicles listing the trust as the owner.

For things without a title, such as jewelry, art, or household goods, use an "Assignment of Property to Trust" or a simple bill of sale.

Small Business Example

If the Smiths own 100 shares in Smith Family LLC, they sign an assignment document (often provided by the company) transferring their shares to the trust.

Documentation, Troubleshooting, and Follow-Up

After each asset is transferred, keep a copy of all deeds, assignments, account paperwork, and confirmation letters. Ask banks or officials for written proof showing the trust is now the owner or beneficiary.

File these records neatly. Not only does this make things easier for loved ones or future trustees, it's proof that your steps worked. Regularly check that accounts, property records, and insurance policies reflect the trust.

Looking Ahead

Careful tracking and following up protect your effort. Mistakes or incomplete paperwork can mean assets slip outside the trust. Knowing what can go wrong—and how to guard against it—will help ensure all the work pays off. Keeping these steps in order lays a strong path for the next phase: recognizing, fixing, and preventing funding mistakes before they cause bigger problems.

Avoiding the Biggest Mistake: Not Funding the Trust

Even after completing the paperwork and creating the trust, many people struggle with the next step—ensuring that the trust truly owns every asset. Creating a trust document by itself does almost nothing if your home, accounts, or life insurance still list you (or your spouse) as the owner. The trust remains empty until the assets are legally transferred. If property stays outside the trust, those assets are not protected or distributed according to your wishes. Instead, they may pass through probate—the public, court-supervised process that you tried to avoid by setting up a trust in the first place. This mistake can erase many of the benefits of estate planning. Even a well-written trust cannot control what it does not own.

Picture a typical situation: A person may spend months with a lawyer detailing their wishes for how a home and savings should benefit the family after their passing, but then they might forget to retitle the house or update the bank account ownership. Later, their children discover the house is still in the parent's name. The trust cannot direct what happens to it, so the court steps in. Probate brings extra costs and risks, delays, and turns private details into public records. Loved ones may have to sort things out through the courts, and assets might not go where you wanted.

Several common pitfalls trip up well-intended trust creators. Many believe that once the trust is drafted, it "automatically" takes charge of everything. That is not true. The trust only controls assets to which it actually holds title or is named as a beneficiary. Others assume assets will switch over by themselves when the trust creator passes away. In reality, without the proper forms and legal steps, accounts and property stay in your individual name, meaning the trust is skipped completely. Some people are unsure which kinds of property need to be moved—does the family home need to be retitled? What about a business, or an old savings account at a credit union? Retirement accounts and life insurance need a special step: updating the beneficiary to the trust or a trust beneficiary, which is often overlooked. One more hidden trap is refinancing a house after transferring it to the trust. Lenders sometimes require taking the property out of the trust to approve the loan, but after closing, the title must be transferred back in—an easy step to forget.

For each of these challenges, a plain strategy can keep mistakes from happening. Keeping an updated checklist of assets is the first move. Write down every account, policy, house, and valuable item, along with whose name is on the paperwork. Then, check each one: Does the title or deed show the trust as the owner or as the beneficiary? If not, ask the bank, broker, insurance company, or county office for their procedure. Never assume a transfer is finished until you have a copy of the new title or a written confirmation from the institution involved. For real estate, review the property deed and make sure it mentions the trust. For retirement accounts and life insurance, get written confirmation of beneficiary changes. This step takes some legwork but prevents trouble for your loved ones later.

Practical routines help keep everything on track. Do an "asset audit" at least once a year, or every time a big change happens, such as buying or selling a house, opening new bank accounts, or getting married, divorced, or having a child. If you move or refinance, review all real estate records again and make sure the trust is still the owner. New assets like cars, business shares, or valuable collectibles should also be considered. When in doubt, ask an institution directly if they see the trust listed as owner.

A simple repeatable plan sets you up for peace of mind:

1. Make and update a master checklist of every asset and account.
2. Audit the checklist after every big life event—new house, refinanced loan, new savings, new business.
3. Confirm the trust owns the asset or is listed as the beneficiary.
4. Keep copies of deeds, account statements, and beneficiary forms in a safe place.
5. Enlist a trusted helper or family member to know where these records are kept.

Sticking to this process gives loved ones the security you intend. By making sure assets are placed in the trust and checking regularly, you prevent court involvement and confusion. Decisions stay private, and your instructions are followed. For parents, homeowners, and business owners, this detailed approach is real protection for the people and projects that matter. Every step completed today spares your family from guesswork and courtrooms later on.

Final Thoughts

Now that you understand the critical importance of fully funding your trust, you can take confident, practical steps to protect your assets and ensure your wishes are honored without unnecessary delays or court interference. By methodically transferring each property, account, and valuable item into your trust and regularly reviewing these details, you create a smooth path for your loved ones to follow, sparing them from confusion, expense, and public scrutiny. This careful attention preserves your legacy and provides peace of mind today, knowing that your estate plan will work as intended when it matters most. With this knowledge, you are ready to move forward and complete the necessary actions that turn your trust from paper into real protection for your family's future.

CHAPTER 18

REAL ESTATE, PROPERTY, AND SPECIAL ASSETS

Have you ever faced the challenge of figuring out how to pass on your home, car, or treasured possessions without leaving your family tangled in legal red tape? Do questions about titles, taxes, and paperwork leave you feeling overwhelmed when planning for the future? Many people want to protect their property and ensure everything goes smoothly after they're gone, yet they aren't sure where to begin or what steps to take. What does it really mean to place real estate, vehicles, or business interests into a trust, and are there items that don't belong there at all? This chapter will guide you through these complex issues with clear explanations designed to help you take control of your assets while avoiding common pitfalls.

Transferring Real Estate and Income Properties into a Trust

Owning real estate brings major benefits, but things can get complicated when it's time to pass those assets to family. Transferring your home and other properties directly into your **trust** allows you to skip probate and give your beneficiaries a clear, hassle-free path to ownership. Instead of waiting months for the court to settle the estate, your loved ones can take over far more easily. You also reduce the risk of confusion or competing claims that sometimes arise when property titles aren't clearly defined after death.

The process starts with a bit of paperwork and a careful review of how your property is currently titled. Here's a typical example: a married couple wants to move their family home into their trust so it passes smoothly to their children. Their first step is to obtain a copy of the **current deed**—the legal document that confirms ownership. This can usually be obtained from the county recorder's office or the title company.

Next, they create a **new deed** that transfers ownership from "John and Susan Smith, husband and wife as joint tenants" to "John and Susan Smith, Trustees of the Smith Family Trust dated May 1, 2022." The legal description of the property must match exactly what appears on the original deed.

A **notary public** must witness the couple signing the new deed—this step is not optional. Counties will not accept or record a deed without notarized signatures. Once signed and notarized, the deed should be submitted for **recording** at the local county office. Some counties charge a small filing fee, but once the deed is recorded, the property officially becomes part of the trust. Once recorded, that office updates public records so everyone can see that the trust is the new owner. To confirm, the couple should request a certified copy after recording and keep it with their trust papers.

Sometimes state laws ask for specific forms or extra steps. In some places, a transfer-on-death deed is an option if you want to pass your home outside probate but are not ready for a full-blown trust. Some homeowners also need to file for property tax exemptions when retitling so these do not get lost in the shuffle. It's wise to contact your local tax office to see if your home needs to be re-approved for any tax breaks, like those for seniors or veterans.

If there's a mortgage on your property, things get a bit more technical. Many lenders include a "due-on-sale" clause in their loan papers, warning that the full balance can be required when ownership changes. Luckily, federal rules often let you move your main residence into a trust without triggering this clause—but it's best to call your lender before making any changes. Homeowners' insurance also needs to be alerted, adding the trust as an "additional insured." This keeps your coverage in place and avoids gaps after the transfer.

Rental homes, vacation cottages, or income properties bring an added layer of steps. When you move a rental house or condo into your trust, the title transfer process mirrors what you'd do for your main home. Start by preparing the new deed, signing and notarizing it, and recording it. On top of this, you must give notice to tenants. This letter explains that while ownership has shifted from your personal name to your trust, the day-to-day rent collection and property rules stay the same. If you use a property manager, inform them so they can update management agreements and payment instructions.

Keep leases and all trust paperwork together to avoid mix-ups. When you update your title, also update landlord/tenant agreements so rent checks go to the trust and rent income is reported under the trust's tax ID. Let's say you own a duplex. After recording the title transfer, you'd send both tenants a short letter with your new "landlord" name, provide the trust's contact information, and confirm any changes to how they pay rent. Update your bookkeeping by listing future property income and expenses under the trust. Make sure your successor trustee can find these records easily.

Numerous problems can lead to obstacles. Forgetting to notify mortgage or insurance companies, skipping notice to tenants, or misreporting rental income on your taxes may complicate things for you and your heirs. Each year, double-check that property taxes and insurance list the trust as the owner. When paperwork, trust names, and real estate descriptions match, you avoid confusion and help the next trustee manage things smoothly.

Checking trust-to-property alignment means that the trust correctly lists every address and property you own. If you inherit or sell property, update the information to keep your trust current. Each scenario—your main home, a family cabin, a rental apartment—comes with its own mix of forms and people to notify. Keeping clear records means your trust remains ready, and makes life easier for whoever steps in after you. Beyond real estate, you will need different steps for vehicles, collectibles, and business interests, each with their own best practices for transfer into your trust.

Including Vehicles, Valuables, Collectibles, and Business Interests

Many families begin their trust planning with real estate, but the same foundation applies when moving to assets like vehicles, valuables, and business interests. Trusts can hold many items beyond a home, creating a more complete safety net that covers a broad range of property and helps your loved ones avoid delays or complications down the road.

How to transfer vehicles

Adding a vehicle to a trust involves changing the legal title to list the trust as the owner. This is not limited to cars—boats, motorcycles, and even recreational vehicles fall into this category. Each type of vehicle comes with its own title and registration, and the steps for transfer generally include:

1. Contacting the relevant agency:

- Cars and motorcycles: Department of Motor Vehicles (DMV)
- Boats: State's boating commission or DMV
- RVs: DMV or specialty vehicle division

2. Completing the agency's title transfer form. Most forms require information about the trust, including its full legal name and sometimes the trust's date of creation.

3. Submitting a copy of the trust (sometimes only a certificate of trust) with the completed paperwork.

4. Paying any transfer fees required by the state agency.

5. Updating insurance to reflect the trust as the titled owner.

If you skip any of these steps, ownership remains with you as an individual, defeating the intent of making your vehicle part of your trust. For instance, when a couple decides to add their family minivan to their trust, they visit the DMV with their trust paperwork and fill out a transfer form, showing both their signatures if the vehicle is jointly owned. After paying the fees, the DMV issues a new title, and the couple then contacts their insurer to confirm the change in ownership on their policy. Boats and RVs follow a similar process, but some states require more involved documentation for specialty vehicles, so checking local requirements is always smart.

Practical points to keep in mind:

- Vehicles with active loans may need lender approval for a title transfer.
- For vehicles used in a business, special rules often apply and may make a trust transfer less suitable.

Including valuables and collectibles

Physical assets that do not have formal titles, such as jewelry, art, coin collections, sports cards, or antiques, require a different approach. These assets get included in a trust through a written assignment or detailed inventory. To provide a clear record, write up a list specifying each valuable item: describe it, note distinguishing features, and include photos or serial numbers. For high-value items like art, an appraisal gives your inventory more weight and supports insurance updates.

Updating insurance is vital when transferring valuables to a trust. Policies may need to match the trust as the legal owner, and values should reflect recent appraisals. Suppose a grandparent wishes to place her emerald necklace, gold watch, and a rare signed baseball card collection in her trust. She lists each item, attaches recent appraisals, and stores photographs with the inventory. Her insurance agent then updates the coverage so that loss or theft is covered, even though the trust is now the legal owner.

Without titles to transfer, the trust relies on your clear inventory. Large items, like antique furniture or sculptures, should get the same treatment: a written assignment, valuation, and updated insurance. Some items, such as collections, benefit from professional appraisals. This builds a stronger case for ownership and helps your trustee make decisions later.

Business interests: steps and cautions

Business interests, such as sole proprietorships, LLC shares, and small business stock, come with unique challenges. In most cases, you assign these assets to your trust through written transfer documents. Here's how the process typically unfolds:

1. Review ownership documents, like articles of incorporation, operating agreements, or stock certificates.
2. Check for transfer restrictions or notice requirements in those documents.
3. Complete an assignment of interest or stock transfer form, naming the trust as the new owner.
4. Update internal business records to reflect the trust's interest.
5. Talk with co-owners or partners, if any, to get their signed acknowledgement or consent, if required.

For example, a small business owner with an LLC reviews her operating agreement and finds a section that requires partner approval for transferring membership shares. After getting approval and signing a written assignment, she updates the LLC records and provides copies to the company's attorney and accountant.

Some states limit the ability to transfer certain types of business stock, or may require special approval from a regulatory body. Always look at the governing documents or speak with a business professional before making changes.

Risks and requirements

Failing to update paperwork, get new appraisals, or follow an agency's requirements can cause headaches later. A car not formally retitled to the trust remains outside the trust and may face probate. An art collection not inventoried might be hard to locate or divide. If a business transfer does not meet company guidelines, co-owners may contest it. Documents and valuations must stay current to guarantee the trust works as intended.

Also, not every asset belongs in a trust. Certain retirement accounts, items with active loans, and vehicles tied to a business may be handled better with other estate planning tools. Understanding these exceptions helps protect what really matters and set up the best plan for each item, leading into a look at assets that work differently or fall outside typical trust planning.

Assets Not Suitable for Trust Inclusion

Business interests, valuables, and collectibles often require special consideration when moving assets into a trust. Each piece has its own rules, paperwork needs, and sometimes, outside legal limits. Missteps in naming or transferring these assets can have lasting ripple effects on your taxes, your heirs, and your overall estate plan. This makes asset selection for your trust just as vital as asset protection. Picking what should stay out is as important as picking what goes in.

Retirement accounts such as 401(k)s and IRAs stand out among popular exclusions. Federal law treats these accounts as tax-protected vehicles tied directly to an individual. Moving a 401(k) or an IRA itself into a trust breaks this chain, causing the account to be "distributed" and taxed all at once. This wave of taxes could erase much of the value you've built over years of saving. A more effective way to fold retirement accounts into your plans is to name your trust as a beneficiary. For example, if your children are young, or if you need to protect a vulnerable adult, naming your trust allows you to direct how and when funds become available. But if the trust gets complicated, such as with multiple beneficiaries or payout rules, required minimum distributions (RMDs) can become tricky or force the account to empty faster than if a person were named. Review these beneficiary choices whenever family or tax situations shift. Double-check that all designations line up with your wider plan, and keep your account paperwork up to date.

Health Savings Accounts (HSAs) and Flexible Spending Accounts (FSAs) bring another wrinkle. Unlike checking accounts or stocks, the IRS only lets a living individual own an HSA or FSA. Ownership by a trust isn't allowed. If you want these funds to help heirs, check if you can name your trust as a final beneficiary. For HSAs, this may work if you want to send any leftover funds to your trust following your passing. Realistically, though, most people use these accounts to zero by the end of their life. Stay on top of rules with your account provider, and have a backup plan if you expect any unused funds—for example, by spending down eligible medical costs or carefully assigning account beneficiaries.

Life insurance policies take a different approach. You may wonder if you should transfer ownership to a trust or simply name your trust as beneficiary. Each path has different results. Naming the trust as the beneficiary means the payout will flow into the trust after you die, where rules you set will guide who gets it, when, and how. This is helpful if your beneficiaries are minor children or rely on special needs care, as it shields the payout from probate and outside claims. If you transfer policy ownership to a trust, though, the rules change; you must watch for gift tax triggers and the "three-year rule" (if you pass within three years of the transfer, the policy may still be counted as part of your taxable estate). For families with children, a life insurance trust can help manage money until those children reach an age you trust them with larger sums. Review your policy's owner and beneficiary lines regularly, and seek advice before making ownership changes.

Certain vehicles, boats, or trailers also deserve attention. These often come with titles and loans, each controlled by state law. Transferring a car or boat with an active loan into a trust may break the lender's rules and, in some cases, prompt them to call the loan due. Also, state laws may block trusts from owning certain vehicles entirely or call for extra paperwork. A practical workaround is the transfer-on-death (TOD) registration, available in many states. With a TOD, ownership passes to a named heir without probate, but you keep normal control while alive. In Arizona, for instance, a vehicle registered with a beneficiary can skip probate, just like payable-on-death accounts do for cash.

When it comes to foreign assets, placing a beach house in Spain or an account in Switzerland inside a US-based trust isn't always possible. Many countries have local ownership, reporting, or inheritance laws that block or complicate foreign property transfers into an American legal structure. Some people set up a separate trust in the country where the property sits or work with international estate planning professionals to create a coordinated solution.

Active business interests and professional licenses present some of the trickiest challenges. LLC memberships with operating agreements, some franchise licenses, or professional practice rights (like law or medicine) might prevent transferring to a trust unless you get approval from partners or regulators. Instead, business succession plans, buy-sell agreements, or naming beneficiaries within company paperwork can provide safe paths forward.

Finally, sentimental items like family photos or childhood drawings are not suited for a trust's asset list, as legal descriptions become unwieldy and open to dispute. Personal property memoranda, or "letters of instruction," attached to a will or trust, let you leave clear handling tips for such items. This gives heirs guidance while keeping your main documents focused and maintainable. Regularly reviewing and updating asset records and beneficiary designations helps avoid most headaches and ensures each asset gets the thoughtful planning it needs.

Final Thoughts

Now that you understand how to manage and transfer various assets into your trust—from real estate and vehicles to valuables and business interests—you're better equipped to protect your estate and simplify the process for your heirs. By carefully following the necessary steps, keeping records current, and knowing which assets should remain outside the trust, you can avoid costly delays and legal complications down the road. With this foundation in place, you can confidently move forward in creating a clear, effective plan that safeguards your family's financial future and ensures your wishes are honored with ease.

CHAPTER 19
TRUSTS, TAXES, AND SAVING BIG

More than half of American adults worry about the costs and complications their families might face after they pass away. Many assume that setting up a living trust will automatically reduce taxes or eliminate legal expenses, but the reality is more nuanced. Understanding how trusts work with taxes and legal processes is essential to making informed decisions that protect your assets and maximize savings for your heirs.

This chapter explains how revocable living trusts relate to income taxes, federal and state estate taxes, and legal fees associated with probate. You will learn why simply transferring assets into a trust does not change your tax responsibilities during your lifetime, how certain strategies can help minimize future tax burdens, and why careful organization and funding of a trust can save thousands in costly court fees. Clear guidance will help you navigate these topics confidently, ensuring your planning efforts translate into real benefits for you and your family.

Understanding Tax Basics and Estate Tax Implications for Living Trusts

Understanding how a **revocable living trust** affects taxes often clears up one of the biggest sources of confusion in estate planning. Many people are relieved to learn that creating a living trust does **not** trigger new taxes, deductions, or exemptions during your lifetime. You remain responsible for reporting and paying taxes on any income the trust's assets generate. Because you retain full control over those assets, the IRS continues to treat the trust as part of your personal tax situation.

For example, imagine a homeowner who transfers their house into a living trust. This change has no effect on how property taxes are assessed or paid. If you currently claim a mortgage interest deduction, you'll continue to do so exactly as before. As trustee (often yourself), you can sell, refinance, or even remove the property from the trust at any time. All income—interest, dividends, rent, or capital gains—is still reported on your regular tax return. During your lifetime, the trust doesn't file its own return because the assets "flow through" to your personal 1040, just as they did before the trust was created.

Looking at other assets, such as investment accounts or bank deposits, the story remains simple. Earnings or gains that these assets produce go straight onto your individual income tax return, using your Social Security number for identification. If your trust investments grow, or if you sell stocks or bonds at a profit inside the trust, that activity is taxed to you, not to a separate trust, as long as your trust is revocable. For most people, the transition is seamless: income, deductions, and tax rates are exactly as they were before the trust.

This brings up a common question: Does putting assets into a revocable living trust lead to lower taxes? The answer is straightforward—no. The trust functions as an extension of you for tax purposes. Its main advantage is helping your loved ones avoid probate court and manage your property if you become incapacitated.

Federal Estate Tax: Do You Need to Worry?

Beyond everyday income tax, many people worry about estate taxes. The federal government collects estate tax only on estates above a certain threshold, and this figure changes occasionally. In 2023, the individual exemption stands at $12.92 million. For a married couple, this doubles to nearly $26 million, as each spouse gets a separate exemption.

Let's look at two families:

- The Sullivans own a home, retirement accounts, and some investments, totaling $500,000. Their estate falls well below the exemption and will not owe federal estate tax.
- The Andersons have $15 million in real estate, investments, and business interests. After the first $12.92 million, their estate could face taxes on the remaining value.

Most Americans—including retirees, parents, single homeowners, and families with blended households—do not reach these exemption limits. Still, a few states collect their inheritance or estate taxes on estates below the federal limit. Some states start taxing as low as $1 million. If you live in one of these states, your estate planner or lawyer can see if those rules apply. These state taxes use different thresholds, rates, and exemptions, so specifics depend on where you live and own property.

Myths About Trusts and Taxes

Myths persist about living trusts and tax obligations. Many believe that forming a trust means your assets "disappear" for tax purposes or that you no longer have to pay estate or income taxes. In reality, a revocable living trust cannot hide or shield you from taxes. You are still the owner, and you must disclose income, pay taxes on profits, and follow all relevant state and federal rules.

Q: Does putting my house in a trust reduce my taxes?

A: No. Mortgage deductions and property taxes are unchanged. You continue reporting and paying as before.

Q: Will a living trust shelter my investments from taxes?

A: No. Dividends, interest, and gains go right onto your personal return. The IRS treats the trust as your alter ego until your death.

Q: Can a living trust help me avoid estate taxes?

A: Not for most people. Unless your estate is above current thresholds, federal estate tax does not apply. The trust avoids probate but not tax.

Building the right legal structure for your assets sets the foundation for efficient tax management. While the revocable living trust itself does not cut your tax bill, strategic planning with trusts and other tools can reduce taxes for your heirs in the future. There are practical trust management options for minimizing tax consequences. These fall into a different category and deserve close attention in the next part of your estate planning journey.

Strategies for Minimizing or Avoiding Taxes Using Your Trust

Understanding when taxes come into play starts with knowing how living trusts are treated. A living trust by itself will not erase all tax bills, but with careful planning, it can help cut down or even avoid certain taxes. Taxes most likely to affect families during life and after death include federal estate taxes, state inheritance taxes, gift taxes, capital gains tax, and tax on any income the trust assets make. Each of these has its own rules and thresholds.

A revocable living trust keeps you in charge of your assets while you're alive. Since you're still in control, the assets stay part of your taxable estate, so there's no reduction in federal estate tax just by making the trust revocable. The real benefit comes with an irrevocable trust. When assets move into an irrevocable trust, you give up control for good. This can remove those assets from your taxable estate, which is a powerful way to lower future estate taxes.

For families worried about federal estate tax, a trust allows you to use what's often called a "bypass" or credit shelter trust. Here's how it works: a married couple can set up a trust so that, when the first spouse dies, a chunk of assets up to a set limit goes into a special trust for the surviving spouse. This amount does not get taxed when the first spouse dies, and when the second spouse passes away, what's left can go tax-free to the kids, up to that same exemption. With federal estate tax exemptions quite high, only those with large estates run into these taxes, but state thresholds can be much lower.

Gift tax comes into focus when transferring wealth to others, such as children or grandkids. With a living trust, you can give away assets without bumping into gift tax, as long as you stay within what's called the annual gift exclusion. For this, you can give up to a set limit each year to as many people as you want without any tax. By placing gifts to different family members inside a living trust, you can spread out the gifts over several years and use up your exclusions while avoiding one-time large gifts that trigger IRS attention.

Many pay attention to capital gains tax when selling property or investments. A big benefit with trusts is the "step-up in basis." When someone passes and the trust distributes the inherited property, the value for tax purposes gets reset to the day-of-death value. This often wipes out unrealized capital gains, so the new heirs can sell the home or other assets and face less tax. It's most useful for family homes, vacation places, and stocks that have gone up in value over time. If a home worth $120,000 in 1990 is worth $500,000 when you pass, your heirs inherit at the $500,000 value, and if they sell soon after, there may be little or no tax.

For those who want to do more than just avoid estate taxes, certain trusts bring extra savings. A charitable remainder trust lets someone leave property to a favored charity while saving on income and capital gains taxes. The way it works: you move appreciated assets, like stocks or property, into the trust. The trust pays an income to you or your loved ones for a certain number of years, and what's left goes to charity. You get a tax deduction up front, income every year, and any capital gains the assets have earned may get shielded from immediate tax.

Generation-skipping trusts shape how and to whom assets pass, skipping over a generation to land with grandchildren. This can dodge large tax bills that would hit if the same assets moved from parent to child, then from child to grandchild, all in two steps. Spreading out wealth this way means more stays in the family.

Trusts with clear "bypass" or "spousal" provisions work well for blended families and second marriages. For example, a parent with children from a first marriage can set up a trust to provide for the new spouse during their lifetime, with the remainder passing to the children from the first marriage later on. This preserves wealth for all intended heirs while controlling both taxes and asset protection.

Pairing a trust with smart use of the annual gift exclusion, life insurance policies, and retirement accounts multiplies savings. For instance, a living trust can hold life insurance or be the beneficiary of an IRA, with careful wording to avoid hitting rough tax territory. Updating trust documents to match tax law changes is always wise to keep the plan on track.

With a well-built trust, families keep things simple, sidestep tax traps, and keep more for the next generation. Choosing the right structure and keeping documents up to date cuts down both taxes and legal costs, freeing up more for loved ones and causes you care about. Families who handle these details carefully see real savings in taxes and time while keeping control over how their legacy is passed on.

Smart Planning to Avoid Costly Legal and Court Fees

Families who plan ahead with living trusts often spare their loved ones more than heartache. They keep them out of the courthouse, away from slow legal processes, and save thousands of dollars in fees. Many people think of trusts only as tax tools, but a living trust's real power lies in how it moves assets without court. Probate court often charges a percentage of estate value for settling someone's affairs, sometimes running from 3% to 8%, not counting extra attorney bills. A home worth $350,000 could mean $10,000–$28,000 in probate costs alone, not even including delays and emotional stress. By moving real estate, bank accounts, and other assets into a living trust, families often keep every dollar for future generations instead of paperwork and commissions.

The key to these savings is aligning legal steps with smart organization. Many people create a trust but do not finish "funding" it. To really skip probate and all related costs, every asset must be retitled. For a home, this means recording a new deed with the county, putting ownership in the trust's name. Bank and investment accounts must officially list the trust as owner. Life insurance and retirement plans need precise, up-to-date beneficiary designations that work together with the trust (or bypass probate themselves). Vehicles, stocks, and personal valuables can also fall under trust control, though local laws matter for certain registration changes.

Setting up this web of instructions avoids court as each institution has everything it needs for simple transfers. Even small errors like a forgotten checking account or car can drag families back into probate for that single asset, causing new attorney visits and paperwork charges. To avoid this, most people use an asset list, updated yearly, as a core trust document. A detailed inventory gives the trustee a map and minimizes court questions later. Here's a checklist to steer clear of missed assets and headaches:

- Place all deeds, car titles, and financial records together
- Review ALL accounts and properties; if in doubt, list it
- Update the trust with any new assets after big life changes (moving, inheritance, sales, etc.)
- Check beneficiary forms yearly, especially after marriages or deaths

A living trust runs smoothly only when loved ones can find everything they need. Many families create careful plans but neglect to say where their documents are. Heirs may spend days (and money) hunting for a will in boxes, or arguing over which binder is up to date. The trust package should always sit in an obvious spot, a labelled folder in a safe, fireproof place, or with a trusted advisor. Sharing access and instructions with successor trustees or a backup family member keeps things easy when the time comes.

Naming a clear successor trustee matters as much as asset lists. Pick someone comfortable with paperwork, who knows family needs, and can communicate well. An alternate or backup is protection against accidents, illness, or family strife. Without named backups, courts may appoint someone and charge extra for the task, adding unnecessary fees. Along with this, give your successor clear directions: a contact sheet, trusted attorneys or financial advisors to call, and a single folder with every important password. This advice turns what can be weeks of legal back-and-forth into a process that takes only days or hours.

Mistakes that trigger extra costs often follow common patterns. People set up a trust but never record a new home deed. Accounts stay in individual names or are partly updated. The trustee may not know they need to inform each bank, insurance company, or title office. Some families miss out on "pour-over" wills that catch leftover assets and funnel them back into the trust. Without these steps, the very court drama people want to avoid comes back, and so do legal and executor bills.

Routine reviews take care of almost every risk. Mark the calendar to refresh asset lists, beneficiaries, and trustee instructions every year or after any life event, a sale, marriage, birth, or death. With a check-in plan, families keep their paperwork tight, minimize surprises, and stick to their goal of avoiding court. For more peace of mind, use easily found guides or checklists from consumer sites, local libraries, or trusted legal document services. Some offer fill-in-the-blank templates for asset lists and funding records that anyone can use.

With these steps, families give themselves more than savings but also speed, privacy, and peace for everyone involved. Careful trust planning means more time spent together and less wasted on legal fights, letting assets move smoothly, just as intended.

Final Thoughts

Now that we understand how living trusts affect taxes and legal costs, we can take confident steps to protect our assets and ease the burden on our families. By carefully organizing and funding a trust, keeping beneficiary designations current, and naming capable successor trustees, you set the stage for smooth transfers without costly probate or surprises. While a revocable living trust won't lower your taxes during your lifetime, smart planning with trusts and related strategies can help minimize tax impacts for your heirs and preserve more of your estate's value. Staying proactive with regular reviews and clear instructions ensures your wishes are honored, your loved ones avoid unnecessary expenses, and your legacy passes on as smoothly and efficiently as possible.

CHAPTER 20

UPDATING AND MAINTAINING YOUR TRUST OVER TIME

When was the last time you reviewed your trust? Do you know if it still reflects your current wishes and family situation? What happens if a major event like marriage, divorce, or a new grandchild occurs and your trust isn't updated to match? Many people create a trust once and then set it aside, unaware that changes in life can make important documents outdated or unclear. How can you be sure your trust will protect your assets and guide your loved ones as you intend? These questions matter because keeping your trust current is an ongoing responsibility, not a one-time task. This chapter will guide you through understanding when and how to update your trust, making sure every change is legally sound, and organizing your documents so they are easy to find and use when needed.

Recognizing When to Update Your Trust and How Often to Review It

A living trust is a living document. Lives shift, families change, and priorities sometimes move in new directions, so the trust that once matched your needs might not fit forever. When a trust becomes out of date, it leaves space for confusion, mistaken directions, family tension, or even the risk that hard-earned assets won't go to the people or causes you care about most. Regularly reviewing and updating your trust helps keep it as reliable and useful as the day it was created.

Major life events call for a close look at your trust. For example, imagine you get married or remarry. It's common to want your new spouse to become a beneficiary, share in certain assets, or even serve in a role such as trustee. Without a revision, a new family member may be left out or roles can be unclear. On the other hand, divorce or the death of a spouse means you may want to remove a former partner from the trust entirely, divide their share among children, or assign new people as successor trustees. This creates clarity and avoids possible disputes.

Adding children or grandchildren is another moment when a trust deserves attention. With the birth or adoption of a child, you likely want to name this new family member as a beneficiary. The trust can also add special conditions for minors, like naming guardians or setting up inheritance terms until kids reach adulthood. Skipping this update may mean new loved ones miss out on protections you intended for them.

If a beneficiary passes away, it becomes necessary to distribute their share in a fair and planned way. For example, maybe a sibling listed in your trust dies before you do. You would then decide how to allocate their share, like giving it to their children or dividing it among living beneficiaries. Careful updates keep your instructions current and lessen the risk of conflict or confusion for others.

Wealth and property also change over the years. Buying or selling real estate, starting a business, or coming into valuable property should lead to a trust review. For instance, buying a second home or a unique piece of art is usually a proud accomplishment, but it can fall outside the trust if not officially included. On the flip side, selling a property or business may mean a trust still lists something you no longer own. This puts your heirs or trustees in a difficult position. Making sure everything you want to pass on is listed, and everything sold or given away is removed, keeps your plan strong and realistic.

Shifts in relationships and intentions often call for updates. Sometimes people grow apart from a trustee or beneficiary, or a blended family forms after remarriage. You might want to support a new charity or modify your legacy to include community organizations that matter to you now. Any of these reasons are valid for making a change. With each update, you keep your intentions front and center and avoid unexpected surprises for loved ones or organizations you care about.

Staying on top of trust maintenance doesn't have to feel overwhelming. Creating a workable routine makes a huge difference. Setting a review schedule puts you in control. Mark your calendar—plan to check your trust every three to five years, and make sure to do it sooner whenever life changes in a major way. Events such as marriage, divorce, welcoming a new child, or buying a home are natural reminders that your trust may need attention.

Some people connect trust reviews with their annual financial check-ups, making it easier to keep everything updated together. Keeping a digital file with your trust and any property records helps you track what might need changing, while a checklist of life events or update prompts can keep you organized. When those changes do pop up, you'll have a clear guide for taking action quickly.

These reviews help prevent confusion and ease stress for your family. When your trust reflects your reality, you save loved ones from having to guess your wishes or sort out missing or outdated information. Regular attention keeps assets safe and ensures the people and organizations you care about are cared for the way you want.

Getting into the habit of proactive review means you are prepared to fix problems before they start. If life brings a change, the trust can keep up. Of course, knowing when to review or update your trust is one thing; knowing how to make your updates legal and clear is the next step. When change is needed, the most pressing question is how do you make sure your trust amendment is official, recognized, and ready to stand up for your wishes?

The Process of Amending Your Trust Document

Life events like marriage, divorce, or the birth of a grandchild make trust review necessary, but review alone is not enough. When a change is needed, amending the trust document makes your new wishes clear, protects your plan's validity, and prevents future confusion. Amending a trust is a formal process, not as simple as jotting a note or crossing off text. The law treats every word in your trust as important, so the path to making changes must stay precise and official.

A trust amendment is an official written document that changes part of your existing trust without replacing the whole thing. This approach works for clear, limited changes like adding a new beneficiary or swapping a trustee. If your changes are widespread, such as changing many beneficiaries, updating distributions, or rewriting the trust's core directions, it makes sense to consider a full restatement. A restatement completely rewrites your trust but keeps the original date and legal identity, making it simpler and reducing confusion for those carrying out your wishes later.

Steps to Amending a Trust

1. Identify the Change

   Think through exactly what you want to adjust. If you intend to add a grandchild as a beneficiary, state their full legal name and date of birth. For removing an ex-spouse, decide if you want to remove just one role (beneficiary, trustee, or both) and clarify this detail. When you want to switch your successor trustee from your brother to your daughter, be sure you choose someone ready for the responsibility.

2. Gather Documents and Information

   Retrieve your original signed trust document. Gather any related existing amendments as well as the details for people involved in your changes, full names, relationships, and addresses if needed. If state law requires certain formatting, get a sample amendment form suitable for your state.

3. Draft the Amendment Document

   The amendment should state that you are the trust's settlor, reference the original trust by its title and date, and clearly spell out which sections you want to change. Avoid ambiguous language. Write, "Article 4, Section B is amended to add: 'John Parker, born May 12, 2023, is a remainder beneficiary in equal shares with the other named grandchildren'" instead of vague language like "add my new grandchild." If you are removing someone as a trustee, specify the article being updated and name the replacement and their alternates.

4. Execution and Legal Formalities

   Please print your amendment and sign it with the same level of formality as the original trust since many states require notarization, and some may request witnesses. If the original trust was signed in front of a notary, do the same for your amendment. Keep signatures clear and complete. Never staple or insert the changes into the original trust; instead, attach the amendment as a separate sheet at the end and label it as "First Amendment to the [Name of Trust]."

5. Organize and Attach Your Amendment

   Staple or clip the amendment to your original trust. Avoid keeping handwritten changes, as these are almost always invalid and create confusion. Only the formal, signed amendment is recognized by the law. Notify your successor trustees and key beneficiaries that you've made an amendment, and tell them where they can find the updated trust document.

Examples to Guide You

When adding a family member, your amendment might look like: "Section 3.04 is hereby amended to include as beneficiary Sarah Williams, born April 10, 2022." To remove an ex-spouse as successor trustee, you could write: "Section 5.02 is amended to remove Jamie Taylor as successor trustee and replace with Mark Taylor."

Key Mistakes to Avoid

- Never write in pen or pencil on your trust document, only signed, witnessed, or notarized amendments are valid.
- Do not forget to reference the specific trust section and use exact legal names.
- Attaching unsigned or incomplete draft amendments will not legally change your trust.
- Failing to notify the relevant parties can lead to disputes or confusion later.

State law determines if witnesses or a notary must be present. Some states allow self-amendment, while others require specific wording or more formal steps. Updates that change your intent for asset distribution or that involve large sums should be reviewed with a lawyer. If you are uncertain, ask an estate attorney to proofread your amendment for accuracy and compliance.

Keeping your amendments together with your original trust is a powerful way to guarantee everyone knows your wishes. As changes become part of your trust history, it becomes just as vital to consider secure storage and clear access for each document so no one is left searching when it matters most.

Keeping Your Trust Documents Accessible and Up-to-Date

Once you have amended your trust and made sure every detail is correct, the real work of protecting your plan begins. The way you store, organize, and periodically review these documents shapes how easily your wishes can be carried out, especially in times of stress or uncertainty. Only you can make sure no one is left searching, questioning, or second-guessing your intentions.

Keeping Your Documents Safe

Trust documents are only as useful as your ability to produce them when needed. The original signed copies carry the most legal weight, so keep these in a fireproof and waterproof safe at home or a bank's safe deposit box. Store backups separately from each other. If you keep the original at the bank, keep a paper or digital copy in another safe location such as your attorney's office or with a trusted relative.

For added protection, scan your documents and save them in a secure online location. Choose an encrypted cloud storage service with strong password requirements and multi-factor authentication. Services like online vaults can also notify you of attempted unauthorized access. Create strong passphrases and consider a reputable password manager to keep login details out of sight but not out of reach. For one family, this might mean original documents in a home safe, copies in a locked file at a sibling's house, and a digital backup accessible only by you and your attorney. If a disaster damages one location, at least one secure backup should remain.

Making the Right People Aware

Documents lose power if no one knows where to find them, or who is supposed to access them. Give clear, written instructions to your chosen trustee and any backup trustees, as well as to your executor. Share the storage location, entry instructions, and any passwords or safe codes they might need in an emergency. Handing over sealed envelopes with access instructions is an option if you want to protect privacy until the right moment.

Still, not everyone needs a full copy of your trust. Only the most trusted individuals such as your designated trustee or attorney should be handed or told about copies. Think of the process like a relay: you pass just enough information to the next person who will need to step in. For families, this prevents frantic calls and rushed searches for documents they never realized existed. If someone needs to act quickly due to illness or a crisis, paperwork is immediately accessible, not locked behind confusion.

Staying Current

A well-kept trust binder or digital file includes more than the trust itself. Life changes like new property, accounts, or family members —happen steadily. It's useful to keep a running asset inventory, updated contact lists for your beneficiaries, and current statements for your major accounts or policies alongside the trust. Create a simple checklist of what you keep and mark a yearly date on your calendar for a review.

When you update your trust, update every related document at the same time. If your trust now names a new beneficiary, your list should match. If you buy or sell property, update the deed references, insurance details, and valuations you store. File everything with the trust, not scattered in different rooms or devices. One effective approach is a binder divided into sections for each type of document, paired with a labeled digital folder with matching names and a backup on a second device.

Sample Annual Review Checklist

- Check original trust and amendments for accuracy
- Update asset list and attach supporting statements for each major asset
- Review and revise contact information for beneficiaries and advisors
- Double-check storage and access instructions for all parties
- Sync paper and digital copies to ensure all versions match

Organizing for Calm and Clarity

A straightforward filing system dissolves confusion. Divide your materials into these groups:

1. Original trust and amendments
2. Certificates of trust
3. Asset lists and inventories
4. Contact lists for trustees, beneficiaries, and advisors
5. Recent account statements or property valuations

Color-code folders or digital folder icons—one color per document group. Add simple, clear labels to each folder or subfolder, along with a brief table of contents or index at the front. Every page or digital file should show its section and date. Consistency lets someone else step in, find what they need, and act fast.

Organization is an ongoing act of care, not a single chore finished for good. Make it a routine, not a burden. Time you invest now means less chaos for those you love and a stronger safeguard for everything you have worked for. Every step you take to secure, share, update, and organize your trust brings peace of mind, not only to you but to everyone depending on a clear, effective plan.

Summary and Reflections

Now that you understand when and how to update your trust, the proper steps to make amendments, and effective ways to keep your documents organized and accessible, you are well-equipped to maintain a clear, reliable estate plan that reflects your current wishes. Regularly reviewing and formally updating your trust ensures your assets are protected and passed on according to your intentions, while careful organization and secure storage prevent confusion and delay for your loved ones. By adopting these practical strategies, you can confidently manage your trust over time, providing peace of mind today and a smoother future for those who depend on your thoughtful planning.

CHAPTER 21
TALKING TO YOUR FAMILY AND TRUSTEES

Have you ever thought about what really happens when a loved one passes and the family has to manage their affairs? How does the person entrusted with these responsibilities know exactly what to do, and how can misunderstandings be avoided before emotions run high? What if the very plan meant to protect your family's future becomes a source of confusion or conflict because no one talks about it openly? These questions highlight why clear communication about your trust is more than just a formality—it's essential for peace of mind and for helping those you care about navigate difficult times with confidence.

Communicating About Your Trust with Loved Ones and Trustees

A living trust is often the backbone of a family's long-term plan, but for many families, even hearing the word "trust" can bring a sense of mystery or worry. Breaking down the purpose and structure of a trust turns that anxiety into something more useful: a shared sense of direction and reassurance. Picture a parent sitting in a comfortable living room, explaining to their grown children, "This trust means that if something ever happens to me, you won't have to struggle with paperwork or wonder what comes next. Our house will stay in the family, and you'll know exactly how everything is meant to work." That kind of clarity grounds everyone. It creates trust in more ways than one.

Explaining these details in simple language helps loved ones understand the real value of a living trust. Instead of locking the legal documents away, open conversation can paint a picture of a future without surprises. The goal is to make sure family members are not blindsided by paperwork or confusion during difficult times. Reassurance might sound as simple as saying, "We created this trust so that the things we've built, like our home, my savings, and the family cabin, are protected. If I'm not here, you still know the plan, and that plan was made with you in mind."

Certain details should always be part of this discussion. Loved ones should know who is named as trustee, what their responsibilities are, when and how they'll need to step in, and which assets are included in the trust. Explain why each person was chosen for their role. For example, "Your Aunt Linda is the trustee because she's good with details and has helped us before with things like this." Connect each choice to familiar strengths instead of making decisions seem random. Talk through how assets will be divided, matching the legal language of the trust to real-life examples. "The savings account is meant for your college expenses, and the house goes to both you and your brother to keep or sell together."

Many families benefit from visual reminders. It helps to have a printed summary or even a hand-scribbled chart showing the main features: trustees, backup trustees, beneficiaries, and main assets. Laying this out together can lock in understanding that reading the document alone does not.

Trustees in particular must receive full and practical information about their role. Keeping a checklist handy makes this more concrete:

Core Information the Trustee Needs

- Location of the original trust and any amendments
- List of all assets included in the trust (such as the house, investments, accounts)
- Contact details for the family's lawyer, financial planner, and insurance agent
- Instructions for handling real estate (for example: maintenance, taxes, insurance)
- Passwords or digital instructions, if assets or accounts are managed online
- Backup trustee's name and contact information
- Calendar of key dates to review responsibilities or distributions
- Any letters of wishes or special instructions not spelled out in the trust
- Emergency contacts and preferences about health or property if incapacitated

Consider a scenario: A homeowner introduces their chosen trustee to the family lawyer during a relaxed lunch. "Let's all meet Attorney Ellis, so if you ever need help, you won't have to introduce yourself when things are stressful." This meeting, organized well before any crisis, removes hurdles. The trustee then knows exactly where to find deeds, titles, and even who to call for property taxes. The family also witnesses a united plan.

Timing matters. Bringing up the trust only during emergencies brings more confusion than comfort. Early and ongoing conversations allow the family to ask honest questions, express worries, and get answers before emotions run high. Start these talks as soon as the trust is finalized, updating everyone if anything changes—such as a new home added to the trust or a change in trustee.

Talking about these topics doesn't have to sound cold or like reading from a legal document. It helps to ground the conversation in care and openness. A parent might say, "I picked you as trustee because I know you're steady when things get busy. I'm sharing all the details not to burden you, but so you feel prepared." Invite questions, promise to revisit any unclear points, and let everyone know the purpose is peace, not pressure. Use clear, short sentences and avoid technical terms unless everyone understands them.

When families talk openly about these plans, they step into the process with less fear and more confidence. Sharing roles, reasoning, and instructions builds unity and prevents stress from boiling up later. What often disrupts trust administration isn't the plan itself—it's confusion, silence, or hidden expectations. The next step involves addressing how to clear up any grey areas or gaps, further cutting down the chance of misunderstanding or disputes.

Preventing Confusion and Legal Disputes Through Communication

Trust plans are designed to protect your wishes and prevent family disputes, but misunderstandings often start when information is vague, assumptions go unchallenged, or intentions are left unsaid. Sometimes all it takes for confusion to spiral is for one family member to learn about a trust for the first time during a stressful moment, or for a trustee to change a detail without explanation. People naturally worry when they're surprised or don't know the reasoning behind choices that affect them.

At the heart of many problems are surprises that catch loved ones off guard. An adult child opening a letter from a bank about their role as trustee, not knowing their parent ever set up a trust, can feel anxiety and resentment even before they read the details. Siblings may find out at a parent's passing that shares aren't what they expected or that a family property is to be managed differently. If we don't discuss these details first, such news frequently results in disputes, accusations, and long-lasting rifts.

Common Situations That Lead to Disputes

Tension often surfaces for several reasons:

- Unclear language in the trust leads each person to a different interpretation about their rights or entitlements.
- Vague explanations or silence leave loved ones guessing at motives and intentions.
- Changes to beneficiaries or distributions are made privately, then revealed later, causing shock or hurt feelings.
- Complex property, like businesses or vacation homes, brings unique questions and assumptions that go unaddressed.

Imagine two sisters who believe they will share their mother's home equally, only to find that one gets full responsibility and the other receives different assets. Without their mother's reasoning explained, suspicion builds. The sister with the house resents the upkeep; the other feels shortchanged. Suddenly, what started as an administrative task becomes a fight over fairness and memory.

In another household, a father talks openly with his children about his trust, explaining he wants each to receive support according to need: one has medical expenses, another is saving for school, and the third is established and receives less. By stating these reasons during his lifetime, answering questions, and writing notes to clarify his thinking, he diffuses resentment before it starts. The trust works as intended, and family bonds endure even after he's gone.

Clarifying Intentions to Lower Tension

Stating intentions openly changes the atmosphere. Rather than leaving beneficiaries and trustees in the dark, lay out your objectives and the reasoning behind key choices. Explain why some assets are distributed equally while others follow a different logic, like supporting a child with extra needs or honoring a family tradition with a certain property. These conversations, though sometimes uncomfortable, shift the tone from secrecy to understanding.

Organizing a family meeting can foster trust and facilitate communication. Use this time to:

1. Invite open questions, including tough or awkward ones.
2. Share the "why" behind decisions—such as the rules about distributing business income or restrictions you've set on selling the family home.
3. Write out the reasoning for decisions that may seem unusual, and keep these notes with your estate files.

For mixed families or complicated property, these steps are crucial. When a family business is part of the trust, explain succession, management rules, and what happens if someone wants to sell. If you've married again and have children from different relationships, consider discussing how you balanced the needs of both families. This prevents disappointment and legal wrangling later.

Supporting Trustees With Guidance and Documentation

For trustees, clear communication is a gift. Lay out responsibilities, timelines, and boundaries so they understand your vision. Make expectations concrete: require regular updates, give a timeline for major decisions, and define when beneficiaries can expect distributions. Written instructions eliminate guesswork and worry.

1. Provide plain-language checklists of trustee duties.
2. Specify how often reports or updates should be shared with beneficiaries.
3. Establish boundaries—such as not loaning trust assets or making side deals so no one feels pressured.

Direct answers to common questions also dispel confusion. Let everyone know who can access what and under which circumstances. If your trust allows for early payouts in emergencies, spell out what qualifies. If disputes arise, set out a process like naming a neutral third-party adviser so small issues don't turn into lawsuits.

Set up regular check-ins or updates, even informal ones, with both trustees and beneficiaries. A short phone call or letter reassures everyone and keeps rumors from spreading.

Lessons from Real Experiences

When clarity is missing, misunderstandings can escalate quickly. For instance, after a parent's death, one brother feels "left out" because the trust splits assets unequally, but the parent never explained why. Arguments follow, fueled by assumptions and old resentments. Legal fees build, communication breaks down, and relationships suffer.

Contrast this with a family in which the parent invites everyone together, explains each part of the plan, and then answers every question. She prepares a short letter outlining her wishes even for assets not detailed in the trust, helping her children understand and remember what matters most. When the time arrives, confusion is low, and the process feels fair.

Extra instructions, sometimes as simple as a letter stating personal wishes, guidance for particular items, or messages about values can go a long way to make sure direction is honored beyond the legal document. With this in mind, families find greater peace, and wishes are more likely to be followed as intended.

Using Letters of Intent or Guidance Documents for Clarity

Writing a trust involves legal rules, which makes the process clear on paper but sometimes confusing in daily life. Beneficiaries and trustees can still feel lost about what the trust creator truly hoped for.

Frustration or disappointment can happen if the legal words do not reflect the personal wishes behind them or leave questions unanswered, especially when it comes to sentimental items, pets, or special gifts. A letter of intent, sometimes called a guidance letter, serves as a plain-language bridge between the legal trust and the creator's intentions. Writing this letter gives you the chance to explain, in your words, the reasons for your decisions removing uncertainty, easing administration, and often preventing conflict.

A letter of intent is not a legal document and is not enforceable in court. Instead, it acts as a supplement to your trust. It puts instructions, explanations, and hopes in a format that trustees and family can understand without needing a lawyer to interpret. The trust lays out who gets what, when, and how. The letter of intent tells the story behind those gifts, clarifies gray areas, and provides guidance for decisions that may come up as the trustee does the actual work.

Core purposes of a letter of intent include helping the trustee settle disagreements or questions, offering reasons for dividing assets a certain way, and describing any special care for pets, dependents, or unique assets that deserve personal attention. The letter can also highlight your wishes for family values or charitable giving. Here are a few core uses:

- Giving practical guidance to the trustee when legal rules leave room for judgment
- Explaining the reasoning behind split or shared assets ("I left the piano for both of you because it belonged to your grandmother, and I hope you work out a way to share or rotate it.")
- Requesting that a family holiday home remain in the family, or that certain traditions continue
- Calling attention to heirlooms, photo albums, or keepsakes with notes about their history
- Asking that a cherished pet receives care from a certain person, with details about routines and needs

A common scenario involves a family recipe box, which has little market value but brings deep emotional memories. The trust may not mention it, so if it goes unspoken, feelings can be hurt. In a letter of intent, you spell out your wish: "I hope the recipe box stays in the family, maybe shared over holidays. I would love for each of my children to add new recipes." Or suppose there is a vacation cabin that has been with your family for years. The legal document might split the property in equal shares, but your letter can add, "I hope you agree to keep the cabin so you can build future memories together." These words do not change the legal force of the trust but give powerful context and guidance for sensitive decisions.

Common elements to include in a letter of intent:

- A list of items with sentimental value and your wishes for them
- Stories or reasons that explain the choices ("This necklace belonged to your mother, and giving it to you means…")
- Clear directions for the care of children, elderly parents, or pets if not set out in the trust
- Ideas for dividing shared property, such as rotating use or holding a drawing for objects not covered by the legal document
- Messages to reinforce family values, traditions, or charitable hopes ("I hope you still volunteer together at the shelter in my memory")
- Instructions about where to find the letter and how often you will update it

Plain language is vital. Write as if you are speaking to your trustee or children directly. Address them by name. Share the "why" behind decisions, especially if something could be misunderstood or cause surprise. Use kind, hopeful wording. Let your trustees and family know where the letter is kept, and remember to update it after major milestones like births, deaths, marriages, or large life changes. A judge cannot enforce the letter, but when trustees receive clear, heartfelt guidance, they often respect the wishes.

For those who want to avoid arguments and confusion, this simple tool makes a big difference. Taking the time to spell out the personal meaning behind gifts prevents second-guessing and reduces tension when your loved ones are already facing a challenging time. The trustee receives support when hard choices come up. Your relatives feel reassured, knowing that your intentions are clear, with your reasoning and stories captured for them to cherish long after paperwork is done.

Final Thoughts

Now that we understand how clear, open communication about your trust helps prevent confusion and conflict, you can move forward with confidence in sharing your plan. By explaining your intentions in plain language, involving loved ones early, and providing trustees with practical guidance, you create a foundation that supports everyone when it matters most. This thoughtful approach not only protects your assets but also strengthens family bonds and provides peace of mind for the future, ensuring your wishes are honored smoothly and respectfully.

CHAPTER 22
WRAPPING IT UP—YOUR LEGACY, SECURED

"Where did I put those papers again?" It's a question many people ask when trying to sort through a loved one's affairs after they are gone. Confusion over scattered documents can lead to delays, disagreements, and unnecessary stress during an already difficult time. Knowing where everything is, and having a clear plan in place, not only eases this burden but also protects what you have built over a lifetime.

Organizing your estate documents is more than an act of tidiness. It is a way to ensure your wishes are honored without confusion or delay. This chapter focuses on bringing order and security to your estate planning so your legacy remains protected, accessible only to those you trust, and ready for whatever the future may bring.

Assembling and Organizing Your Essential Estate Planning Documents

A trust binder, sometimes called an estate planning folder, brings together your most important legal documents in one organized place. Its main purpose is to make your wishes easy to follow, reduce confusion for your loved ones, and simplify the job of your chosen helpers, such as your trustee or executor. When the need arises, those managing your affairs won't waste time searching or risk missing critical paperwork. Everything needed is on hand, clear, and ready to put your plans into action.

Every strong trust binder starts with the signed original of your living trust and a few clear, readable copies. This legal document spells out what happens to your property and belongings. It appoints the person who will manage the trust, explains how debts get paid, and directs exactly who inherits what, and when. Having the original and a few copies ensures there's always a backup for court filings or when multiple people, like co-trustees and financial advisors, need access at once. For example, if you own a vacation house, your trust may say the house goes to your children, with clear terms for upkeep or sale. Without an organized trust and copies ready, delays and disputes can follow.

Next comes the pour-over will. While your trust covers the assets titled in its name, the pour-over will acts as a safety net. It scoops up any assets accidentally left out of the trust such as a forgotten bank account or car title, and directs them into the trust after your lifetime. For a property owner or small business owner, this is essential. If you buy a rental home but don't retitle it in the name of the trust, the pour-over will ensure that property goes into the trust, avoiding a drawn-out court process.

For control during life, two types of powers of attorney should always be included, each with originals and backup copies. The financial power of attorney covers everything from paying bills to handling investments. If you become ill or injured, your chosen financial agent can step in right away. This prevents court intervention and protects everything from your checking account to your rental property management. The medical or healthcare power of attorney lets a trusted person make medical decisions if you cannot speak for yourself. For families with aging parents or caregivers, having these powers organized and available means no one is left guessing during big life moments.

Add the advance healthcare directive or living will. This spells out your wishes for medical care if you're unable to communicate, such as end-of-life treatment or life support. For parents who want to spare their children from making tough medical decisions, this doc provides clarity and prevents family arguments. The medical team and your appointed agent get instant direction, avoiding unnecessary suffering or confusion.

A certification of trust, sometimes called a trust summary, belongs in the mix too. This brief document proves your trust exists and has authority, but it doesn't reveal your private wishes. Banks and real estate agents often want to see this before letting a trustee move money or sign papers for a property sale. Business owners or real estate investors use this summary to open new accounts or transfer property titles under the trust's name, all without exposing every detail.

Maintaining a current list of trust assets is vital. This inventory includes things like home and deed papers, car titles, bank and investment account statements, life insurance policies, and small business documents. Each entry should be backed up by copies of relevant paperwork. When the time comes to administer your trust, your trustee can act quickly rather than hunt for hidden accounts. For example, someone who owns a franchise can include licensing paperwork, making any future transfer smoother.

Beneficiary designations on retirement accounts or life insurance require their attention. The binder should have clear copies of completed forms and receipts or online confirmations. This guards against errors or missing funds, since financial companies will pay out based on these documents, not your trust or will. Suppose a parent intends that life insurance benefits go to a child's guardian; keeping the forms visible in the binder helps everyone stay aligned.

Strong organization keeps it all working. Use labeled tabs or dividers for each document type. Include a checklist summarizing what's inside and what's missing. Store a digital copy on a secure drive or in the cloud, using password protection. Back it up on a physical drive held in a fireproof safe. Regularly update both paper and digital copies whenever you change accounts, add property, or update wishes.

Round out the binder with contact lists for your attorney, CPA, financial planner, and insurance agent. Include copies of all current insurance policies. A list of digital assets—like online accounts, cloud backups, and social media profiles—and written login credentials with clear directions lets your helpers manage or shut down accounts as needed. For parents or caregivers with online photo libraries, password access lets memories stay in the family.

Storing everything together builds confidence and protects your legacy from legal confusion. This process also demands smart decisions about who can access your sensitive information and where everything is physically kept, setting up a smooth move into privacy and security planning.

Safeguarding Privacy and Peace of Mind in Estate Planning

With all your trust binder's pieces in place, privacy steps in as the partner to the organization. Careful recordkeeping turns into real protection only when sensitive details remain out of the wrong hands. Every person handling an estate leaves a trail of private data account numbers, social security numbers, passwords, insurance details, healthcare facts, and even physical property records. This information, if exposed, can invite everything from annoying spam to the nightmare of identity theft, drained bank accounts, or even scams targeting your heirs.

The kind of details that deserve extra attention include social security numbers, birth certificates, driver's licenses, bank account numbers, credit card details, property deeds, health insurance information, and logins for digital accounts. A shared computer, loose papers on a desk, or careless sharing can all lead to trouble. Identity theft remains one of the leading risks, often carried out when someone gathers enough information — an account number here, a digital password there — to impersonate a person, take out loans, or drain accounts. Addresses or phone numbers shared without protection frequently result in junk mail and unwanted calls.

A solid privacy plan starts with storage. Physical documents live best in locked, fireproof boxes at home. Safe deposit boxes in banks add another level for anything you rarely need but want to keep extra secure, such as original wills or property deeds. Make sure these are not left where visitors, cleaning staff, or anyone outside your trusted circle might glance at them. Share the location and access instructions with only a couple of people you trust absolutely, such as a spouse or legal representative. Over-sharing reduces security.

When it comes to digital files, create unique, hard-to-guess passwords for each folder or file containing personal details. Do not use predictable combinations - no birthdays, pet names, or repeated strings. Password managers can help generate and store complex passwords. Encrypt digital documents by using built-in file encryption tools or setting passwords for sensitive PDFs and word processor documents. If you choose cloud storage, pick a provider known for solid security, including two-factor authentication and strong privacy terms. Example: after writing your will, you scan and save a copy in an encrypted folder on Google Drive. Set a strong password, and only share it with your executor.

Access should always match your situation. If a divorce or new marriage changes your circle of trust, update who knows the combinations, passwords, or even the location of key files. Neglecting this step can leave former partners or even estranged relatives with too much power or trusted new people with none. Review your permissions every year or whenever relationships or responsibilities change.

Communicating safely matters as much as storage. Never send passwords, social security numbers, or bank details through plain email, texts, or social messaging. These can be intercepted or forwarded with a few careless clicks. When you need to transfer sensitive documents, consider these options:

- Secure online portals often used by attorneys and banks
- Physical hand-off—giving originals or copies to others in person
- Certified mail with delivery alerts for important paper documents
- Password-protected digital attachments, with passwords shared by phone rather than email
- Two-factor authentication for online platforms

Everyday habits also play a big role. Avoid using shared family computers to store or edit financial files. If you must, create a separate, password-protected profile and never save passwords or files to the desktop. Backups matter—if your laptop dies or your home experiences a break-in, you don't want to lose everything or find it's now in the wrong hands. But think hard about who gets the backup. Trusted adult children, legal counsel, or a second executor may be candidates. Avoid including unrelated friends or business partners in your backup plans to prevent confusion or disputes if something happens to you.

Examples cut through confusion. Imagine a woman who kept her trust binder on her bookshelf, visible to guests. When a neighbor's curious child opened it, a stray paper was lost and later mishandled, leading to calls from scammers weeks later. This could refer to a family that failed to update the ex-spouse's access to online banking, leading to the discovery that assets had quietly vanished following a sudden illness.

Privacy becomes even more effective when it's a family affair. Teaching your trusted representatives how and why files are protected lets them keep your wishes secure while responding confidently on your behalf. Walk them through the process of how to access files, who they can share with, and what never to communicate by regular email or social media. This reduces future mistakes and speeds up needed actions during emergencies.

Before your binder is declared done, take a moment. Review each method of storage, sharing, and updating to make sure your information remains safe. Keeping these steps in mind means your legacy stays protected from both accidental and purposeful threats, paving the way for the last checklist that brings every loose end together.

The Ultimate Living Trust Success Checklist

When every important document sits snugly in its folder, privacy turns from theory into real protection. Families who keep trust files organized and secure avoid chaos, lost files, and needless worry. Taking time now to double-check every step locks in peace of mind.

Step-by-Step Living Trust Finalization Checklist

- **Examine Each Page for Accuracy and Completeness**

    Compare all trust documents with the most recent information about your assets and wishes. Names, dates, and addresses must match exactly—spelling errors or outdated contact information can delay or stop your plans in court.

    Tip: Use a highlighter to mark spots you're unsure about and return to them with fresh eyes or with a helper.

    Even small omissions like a missing initial, unsigned page, or extra blank space can cause trouble for your family at the very time they need support the most.

- **Retitle Real Estate and Financial Assets to the Trust**

  Make sure each property has its deed clearly signed over to the trust.

  Example: For a family home, the county records must show the trust as the new owner of the property, not an individual's name.

  Do the same for bank accounts, investment funds, and business interests. Call the bank and ask for the trust transfer paperwork. Get all confirmation letters in writing.

  Common pitfall: Skipping this step leaves assets outside the trust's protection, often resulting in probate and argument among heirs.

- **Gather and Organize All Supporting Legal Documents**

  Place your will, powers of attorney, advance healthcare directive, property schedules, beneficiary lists, and any guardianship designations together in a single, clearly labeled binder or folder.

  Maintain both physical and digital copies whenever possible. Use password-protected files stored in secure cloud storage or on an encrypted external drive.

  Useful tool: Color-coded file dividers or folders make finding each document faster under stress.

- **Secure Storage and Reliable Access**

  Store original signed documents in a fireproof safe, bank safe deposit box, or locked file cabinet with restricted access.

  Choose two to three trusted people (successor trustees, agents, spouse, attorney) and ensure that they either know how to access these documents or hold a copy.

Do not rely on a single location, as disasters or technical failure can leave your family stranded.

• Keep Track of Digital Accounts and Access Information

List every online banking, retirement, investment, crypto, and document storage account attached to your estate. Write down account numbers and access instructions, and store these with your trust documents.

If passwords change, update the list immediately.

Provide clear written instructions on how to recover or access each account.

Tip: Use a secure password manager and include the master password on paper, sealed in the file for your successor trustee.

• Communicate Roles and Document Locations to Key People

Speak directly with your successor trustees, agents, and main beneficiaries. Show them where documents live and walk them through their responsibilities.

Give a printed "cheat sheet" with contact information, safe combinations, or access codes.

Avoid the problem of secrets—confusion and disputes can pop up fast when people don't know where to look or what you wanted.

• Set Up a System for Regular Reviews

Plan to revisit your documents every two or three years, and after major life events like births, deaths, marriages, divorces, new investments, or property sales.

Adjust property schedules and beneficiary lists as your circumstances shift. Use a calendar reminder or a checklist app to stay on track.

Tip: Keep a simple review log with the date, notes, and any changes made.

- **Document Every Action, Change, and Communication**

  Record when assets are retitled, passwords updated, people notified, or legal advice received. Write this in a bound notebook or a digital spreadsheet.

  This record will save time for successors who want to show that everything was handled according to your wishes.

- **Check for Complex or High-Value Asset Issues**

  Businesses, out-of-state property, intellectual property, or large investments might need a lawyer's eye. If anything feels confusing or high stakes, get a review from a qualified estate attorney. A small check now can prevent months of conflict later.

Sample Trust File Organization

- Living trust document (original, signed)
- Property deeds retitled to trust
- Financial account transfer letters
- Schedule of assets
- Will and powers of attorney
- Advance healthcare directive
- List of digital accounts and passwords (sealed)
- Communication cheat sheet for trustees
- Review and action log

Staying organized and proactive means heirs can skip headaches, speed through the legal process, and focus on honoring your wishes. Every item checked off secures your estate's future and protects your loved ones from confusion and disputes when it matters most.

Bringing It All Together

Now that you have a clear roadmap for assembling, organizing, and securing your estate planning documents, you can move forward with confidence that your legacy is protected. A well-prepared trust binder, combined with strong privacy measures and regular reviews, ensures your wishes are honored smoothly and without unnecessary delays or disputes. Taking these practical steps today means your loved ones will be spared confusion and stress tomorrow, allowing them to focus on what truly matters—preserving your family's future and peace of mind.

YOUR VOICE CAN SAFEGUARD SOMEONE'S FUTURE

Every step we take to plan ahead becomes a gift of peace of mind for those we leave behind.

Have you ever paused to think about what would happen to your family, home, and assets if something unexpected occurred?

Imagine a loved one suddenly facing complicated court proceedings, mounting legal costs, and unnecessary stress simply because no clear living trust was in place. Your reflections on this book and what you've learned about living trusts could inspire others to protect their families before it is too late.

If this book helped you understand how a living trust works, organize your estate with greater confidence, or feel more at ease about your family's future, I would be truly grateful if you shared a short, honest review. Your feedback supports my work and serves as a guiding light for someone who may be standing where you once stood—unsure, anxious, but ready to safeguard what matters most. Even a few sentences can ripple outward, helping others take charge of their legacy with clarity and peace of mind.

Thank you for reading, reflecting, and being part of this journey. Your words may carry more impact than you realize.

CONCLUSION

There's a quiet reassurance that comes when you know you've taken steps to protect what matters most. After reading this book, you're far better equipped than most people. You understand what a living trust is, how it can guard your wishes, and why it's one of the most powerful but straightforward tools for securing your family's future.

A lot of people worry about estate planning—some feel it's too complicated, others think they don't have enough assets to bother, or maybe they've heard horror stories about probate court dragging on for months or even years. If any of these concerns sound familiar, you're not alone. These fears are understandable, especially given the confusion that often surrounds estate planning and wealth transfer. But here's the truth: setting up a living trust isn't reserved for the ultra-wealthy or legal experts. It's an act of care, clarity, and foresight open to anyone who wants to offer their loved ones peace of mind and certainty.

The core benefit of having a living trust in place is simple: it gives you control. You choose how your assets are handled, who receives them, and under what conditions. Instead of leaving things to chance—or to unpredictable court processes—you create a clear path for your home, savings, and cherished belongings. For homeowners, this means your property can pass directly to your family or chosen heirs without being tied up in the probate system, which can be expensive, invasive, and time-consuming.

Middle-income families especially stand to gain. The costs of probate are often disproportionate to the value of the estate, eating into inheritances and delaying closure at a difficult time. With a living trust, those expenses can be avoided almost entirely. Your family won't have to deal with mountains of paperwork or pay out thousands in legal fees just to claim what you intended for them. They'll also avoid the public records process, maintaining privacy during a sensitive period.

For parents and grandparents, a living trust is a real gift to those you love. It's not just about money—it's about making transitions easier, keeping your intentions crystal clear, and even protecting young beneficiaries until they're ready to manage assets responsibly. If you've spent years working hard for your family, a trust ensures your efforts continue to support them, no matter what happens next.

If you're caring for aging parents, or guiding them through their own estate planning, the ideas in this book will help you ask the right questions and avoid common mistakes together. Acting now, before a crisis or illness, means sidestepping confusion and heartache later.

And if you're a young professional or small business owner just starting to accumulate assets: there's no downside to early planning. A living trust can be updated as life changes. Marriage, children, new properties, or a growing business—all can be addressed in the trust as your circumstances evolve. Starting now sets a stable foundation, giving you freedom to focus on the future.

Maybe your situation involves a blended family, stepchildren, or dependents with unique needs. Clarity is essential in these cases, where generic wills or intestacy laws (what happens if you don't have a plan) may not reflect your wishes at all. A living trust allows you to spell things out precisely, minimizing conflict and potential challenges after you're gone.

Throughout this book, we've broken down the steps to creating a living trust using simple, modern language—no legal jargon, no unnecessary technicalities. The process might seem daunting at first, but by approaching it in manageable pieces, you can steadily move forward. Remember: you don't have to do everything all at once. Even small actions taken today—making a list of your assets, thinking about your trusted decision-makers, talking with your spouse or children—can set the wheels in motion. Each step reduces the risk of confusion later and increases security for your family.

Many people put off estate planning, promising themselves they'll get to it someday. Yet the unexpected can happen at any time. By acting now, you're taking charge of your story while you still have every option available. You're protecting your legacy, your loved ones, and yourself from unnecessary stress.

Sometimes, the hardest part is just getting started. If you've read this far, you've already accomplished more than most. You've carved out time to educate yourself and demystify a subject that can feel intimidating or overwhelming. That's a victory worth celebrating. You've closed the knowledge gap, and now, you're poised to close the action gap as well.

You do not need to finish everything overnight. Set a realistic timeline; give yourself permission to go at your own pace. Perhaps you begin with a short meeting with your partner to discuss priorities. Or maybe you draft a simple outline of your wishes. Every effort counts. Over time, these small steps come together to form a robust plan—a safety net woven lovingly for your family.

If you prefer a hands-on approach and want to minimize attorney involvement, there are practical resources and guides available. This book's approach is designed for DIY-minded individuals, empowering you with checklists, sample documents, and explanations in plain English. You may find that, having learned the basics, you feel comfortable handling a great deal yourself and only need professional input for specific questions. That puts you fully in the driver's seat, saving both time and money.

If you do decide to consult an attorney, you'll be able to communicate clearly, ask informed questions, and insist on transparency throughout the process. That kind of confidence is invaluable, ensuring you receive the service and results you deserve.

Most importantly, with a living trust in place, you remove much of the uncertainty and anxiety that so often surrounds end-of-life matters. You give your family the enormous gift of clarity. No guessing games, no searching through boxes for forgotten documents, no family friction over ambiguous instructions. Instead, you leave behind a roadmap, tailored to your values and goals, that enables your loved ones to grieve, remember, and ultimately move forward with compassion and understanding.

As you close this book, take a moment to recognize your accomplishment. You've gained knowledge that will ripple outwards, benefitting everyone you care about. The peace of mind you create is not just for yourself, but a lasting legacy that will echo through generations.

Secure your future by putting your plan into action. Protect your home, your savings, your family, and your story—while you have the power and presence of mind to do so. Start today. Small steps lead to big rewards, for you and for everyone who depends on you. Peace of mind truly does start with a plan—and now, you have everything you need to make yours a reality.

www.ingramcontent.com/pod-product-compliance
Lightning Source LLC
Chambersburg PA
CBHW050524240926
51846CB00003B/677